LOOK UP

Look Up

Defying All Odds with God's Faithfulness

Trina Powers-Hadley

©2025 All Rights Reserved. No portion of this book may be reproduced, stored in a retrieval system, or transmitted in any form or by any means—electronic, mechanical, photocopy, recording, scanning, or other—except for brief quotations in critical reviews or articles without the prior permission of the author.

Published by Game Changer Publishing

Cover Design: Skylar Ringenbach

Cover Photo Courtesy: Carrie Lynn Dodson

Paperback ISBN: 978-1-966659-77-8

Hardcover ISBN: 978-1-966659-78-5

Digital ISBN: 978-1-966659-79-2

www.GameChangerPublishing.com

DEDICATION

This book is dedicated to all of those who have aided in Shane's Glory to God story. To every family member, friend, rodeo family, medical staff, acquaintance, or stranger. Any that helped physically, monetarily, at home or afar, emotionally or spiritually, especially all the people who lifted us up in prayer. Faith, belief, love, care, and prayer sustained us, and we have so much thanks and gratitude for standing in agreement! Words cannot express our sincere appreciation. We send up prayers of thanksgiving for each of you and send our love in Christ to you all.

IN MEMORY

This book is in memory of those young loved ones we lost too soon: Heather Shane Felts, my niece. Griz Johnson, Jim's nephew. Colleen's and RC's son, Ryan Christopher Donaldson. My shared birthday twin, Stevie Smith, whose family friendship goes back three generations. Aaron Custer, the son of my brother in Christ, Cody Custer.

And to my namesake, Eddy Shane, whose mother, Annette, and I have shared a friendship for over five decades. As the mother of Eddy Shane, she wants us to know that it is not God's will to take our young ones away. He picks them up and carries them home because all His promises are in Heaven.

Heather, Griz, Ryan, Stevie, Aaron, Eddy, and so many others… Rest in peace until we see you again.

READ THIS FIRST

To say thanks for buying and reading my book, I invite you to visit looktofaith.com for a chance to put faces to the names of some of the wonderful people involved in Shane's healing journey. The website is dedicated to his nonprofit foundation. There, you can click on the *Look Up* book extras to view photos from his actual journey.

In addition, you'll find the foundation's mission statement and scriptural encouragement for the future. Shane's attitude of hope reminds us that we are blessed to be a blessing—helping those in need, just as he was helped. He is truly motivated to live out Galatians 6:2: *"Bear one another's burdens, and so fulfill the law of Christ."*

Scan the QR Code

LOOK UP
DEFYING ALL ODDS WITH GOD'S FAITHFULNESS

TRINA POWERS-HADLEY

"But I will sing of Your power; Yes, I will sing aloud of Your mercy in the morning; For You have been my defense And refuge in the day of my trouble."
—Psalms 59:16 NKJV

ACKNOWLEDGMENTS

"I have been friends with Jim Hadley for over 50 years. When I think of Shane, I remember watching him bulldog a tough-necked, sour-tempered, 750-pound, roped-out, three-year-old roping steer. He wrestled with that steer for what seemed like two minutes but never quit. Exhausted and out of breath, he finally threw him down. He was all in.

I see Shane all in on the Word of God, his faith, sharing the Word daily, family, riding, roping, and working cattle. He is just a good guy—all in, all around, no matter what life throws at you."

—Dennis Motes, PRCA World Champion Team Roper

"Over 30 years, I watched (Trina) love her family with a devotion that seemed almost fearless. But when life dealt the Hadley family unimaginable hardships—losing their Wyoming ranch, battling cancer and Parkinson's, and then facing Shane's near-fatal rodeo accident—Trina's faith never wavered. This book is more than a story; it's a testament to the power of faith, resilience, and an unshakable belief in God's promises.

Like Job from the Bible, the Hadleys refused to give in to doubt or despair. Shane's staggering battle for recovery defied all odds, proving that miracles happen when faith is stronger than fear. As someone who has also fought to survive against dire medical predictions, I know the power of unwavering belief and the impact of those who stand in the gap for us. Look Up is a guidebook for overcoming the darkest moments of life, a reminder that no matter how deep the valley, there is always hope. Trina's relentless faith kept her family alive—against all odds—and this book will inspire you to do the same."

—Julie Mankin, Published Writer, Wyoming Cowgirl,
Friend and Fellow Survivor

"I am honored to have met Shane and his family shortly after his severe traumatic brain injury (TBI). I have continued to guide, advocate for, and provide resources to Shane throughout his brain-healing journey. Shane is an extraordinary man. His steadfast dedication and commitment to healing have never wavered. His faith in God has kept him moving forward through the long and arduous rehabilitation process necessary to achieve the healing he so desires. His positive, never-quit attitude is contagious and inspiring to those of us privileged to witness his miraculous recovery.

Shane remains deeply committed to his recovery, and the unwavering support of his family has been both incredible and instrumental. His deep-seated desire to share his story and help others is a testament to the man he is. This book will provide hope to many who may not believe that brain healing is possible. I am grateful to know Shane Hadley."

—Jill Cde Baca, Co-founder of a Non-Profit Foundation focused on the healing of sports-related brain injuries and concussions

"Shane Hadley is simply a living 'miracle.' His will and determination to overcome all odds is a true inspiration. Toughness, courage, fight, and a heart as big as they come are just the tip of the iceberg when it comes to Shane. I'm beyond blessed to call him my friend."

—Coach Bill O'Boyle, Offensive Line Coach for Northwestern University

"I have known Shane since he was a young boy. He has always been a person who embodies the cowboy spirit... tough, dedicated, determined, and a never-give-up attitude. I have no doubt that Shane will continue to defy the odds, and his faith will keep shining through."

—Birch Negaard, 10x NFR Steer Wrestler, 2003 Reserve World Champion Steer Wrestler, Badlands Circuit Steer Wrestling Champion, Columbia River Circuit Steer Wrestling Champion, 2000 Pendleton Roundup All-Around Champion and Steer Wrestling

"People who have never experienced the loss of a child, a young family member, or the accidents that cause such losses, haven't a clue about the pressure—mentally, morally, or financially—that it creates. We often turn to Faith, or derivatives of God, expecting a total recovery, and that can be hard to find. We need to share both the highs and lows of our experiences with others so that when they face tribulations, our hearts can strengthen theirs. Take time to cherish the moments of love you've had and expect even more to come. May all who read this note of love understand that time spent in loving moments with others is time well spent—and everyone wins!"

—Bob Tallmann, Family Friend and PRCA Hall of Fame Announcer

"I enjoy the privilege of a close friendship with the Hadleys. They are an inspirational family, and I have watched them not only talk the talk, but also walk the walk. In Look Up, Trina's detailed account of her son Shane's life—before, during, and after his tragic rodeo accident—proves that an attitude of unwavering faith in God's promises can lead to miracles, both great and small. This book is brimming with hope and conveys the powerful message that faithful belief in answered prayers is the stance God wants us to take. The Hadley family, by faith, has spoken Shane's miraculous recovery into reality.

Being no stranger to severe rodeo accidents myself—having suffered three broken necks during my 35-year rodeo career—I understand the necessity of leaning on God's promises for healing. As Jeremiah 33:3 says, 'Call to Me, and I will answer you, and show you great and mighty things, which you do not know.' This book, with its faith-filled message, deserves a wide readership."

—Rob Smets, 5X World Champion Bullfighter

"I have known Shane and the Hadley family my entire life. Our families neighbored each other in Crook County, Wyoming growing up, and they are some of the best Cowboys/Ranchers we know. I have watched Shane grow up rodeoing and doing sports and always thought he was one of the toughest cowboys and athletes I have seen. Just when I thought he couldn't get tougher, he does things most cowboys would have given up on. Shane shows the true meaning of 'Cowboy tough' even after his accident. I have never once seen him feel sorry for himself or ask for any handout. To me, he's the definition of a true Cowboy."

—Chancey Williams, Country Music Singer/Songwriter and Recording Artist

"Shane is a walking testimony of undying faith and unwavering belief that remained strong regardless of his circumstances or challenges—the kind of faith that doesn't falter, even when faced with adversity or uncertainty. This type of faith is rooted in his strong conviction and trust in someone greater. When doctors said he would never walk again, he chose to give it all to God and trust in His divine power. Shane's story is a true miracle, and it continues to provide hope and reinforce faith in those around him, reminding them that there is a greater force at work—one capable of bringing about positive change in seemingly impossible situations."

—JJ Hampton, 18x World Champion Cowgirl and National Cowgirl Hall of Fame Inductee

"I have been a dear friend of the Hadley family for over forty years. Through the grace of God, consistent prayer, and faith greater than a mustard seed, I have witnessed their determination, family, hope, love, and sharing this beautiful journey with their son Shane. Shane's story is so much more than uplifting, and the title Look Up is something we should all do more of."

—Shelly Burmeister-Mowery, National Cowgirl Hall of Fame Inductee and Former Equine Sports Broadcaster

"I've witnessed a miracle take place in the lives of the Hadley family. I never had a relationship with them before the accident, but met them sometime afterward. I knew about the wreck and prayed for them. When we met, we immediately formed a strong connection because of our mutual faith and trust in the Lord. As is often the case, other people's stories can impact our lives—if we choose to be a part of them.

Shane loves God and people, and it shows every time I see him. Trina and Jim are great examples of how to love God as well as people, which, according to Scripture, are the two greatest commandments."

—Cody Custer, World Champion Bull Rider

"If you are a believer—pick up this book. If you are not a believer—pick up this book. If you are in the best time of your life or at the bottom of the pits, you need this book in your life. Knowing Trina and the Hadley family personally, I have witnessed their undeniable faith and unwavering belief. Watching the tribulations they have faced is difficult for those around them, but at every stage and in every trial, this family stands as a testament to the power of speaking the truth and believing with your whole heart. Trina offers an incredible look into their world, the mountains they have climbed, and their amazing testimony. This family, their journey, and the gift of this book to the world will change your life—and if not, it will certainly change your outlook."

—Laura Lambert, COO Morpheus Media,
Publisher for *On SI*, a division of *Sports Illustrated*

CONTENTS

Introduction	xxi
1. Doing Life	1
2. Let's Rodeo! Kinda…	13
3. You Think You're Good, But Be Better	21
4. Stay Hooked	37
5. In The Boogie	51
6. I See You 51	65
7. We're Out of Here	87
8. Don't Weaken Now	95
9. Surrender All	105
Conclusion	119
Thank You For Reading My Book!	123

INTRODUCTION

"Now when these things begin to happen, look up and lift up your heads, because your redemption draws near."
–Luke 21:28

Having the last name Powers, I grew up with a deep sense of purpose—powerful, just as the name suggests. Raised in a family lineage of Baptist preachers, I was filled with awe and a strong connection to God. To add to that sense of wonder, our family can trace its roots to the legendary Daniel Boone, which only deepened my sense of identity and heritage.

Alongside this spiritual foundation, I was also raised as a cowgirl. That left room for a spirit that was wild and untamed—yet it was also learning, in its own time, the responsibility that comes with being a child of the Most High God. This journey has led me to become an unapologetic, Jesus-loving Christian.

Born into a ranching and rodeo family, my father was one of the founding Turtle Members of the now-renowned Professional Rodeo Cowboys Association. This heritage defined me—not only as a competitor in roping events but also as someone who helped raise, care for, and tend to cattle. I am grateful to be a cowgirl in every sense of the word.

I am blessed to be the wife of Jim Hadley and the mother of Shiloh and Shane. The greatest joy of my life is my four grandchildren, made possible by their dad, our handy cowboy son-in-law, Andrew Napp. I pray to be a

INTRODUCTION

humble yet powerful witness, friend, warrior, and survivor, giving all glory to God.

By God's grace, I have survived against extreme odds. There have been so many times when the statistics were against me, yet here I stand—a living testimony of God's faithfulness. This is due, in part, to the guidance of my parents, Louis and Jayne Powers, who surrounded me with unwavering love, godly influence, and steadfast faith. Without my total belief in God, Jesus, the Bible, and the promptings of the Holy Spirit, none of my success would have been possible.

It's that faith—hope, trust, and a never-quit, cowgirl-grit attitude—that fuels my determination today. My mission now goes beyond me. I am fighting to beat the odds of ovarian cancer, not just for myself, but for others who need to see that they, too, can overcome. I want to be an encouragement to others, to show them that they can be used by God to witness His power, to lead in hope, and to live life fully, as Jesus died and rose again to give us the opportunity to do.

This book is not just a story of a cowboy's accident; it is proof of what God can do when we release faith that He is able. God's promises are true yesterday, today, and forever. Miracles still happen in modern-day life, but they begin with the belief that they can. These words are for anyone who has lost hope, for anyone who needs to believe in the face of impossible circumstances.

If you've lost your hope, if you're struggling to believe when there's no physical evidence to support it, this is for you. It's also for those who may be angry with God, those who blame Him for their suffering. What matters here is not my story but God's truth and an opportunity for you to see the evidence of what God has done in our lives, through our faith. It is also about equipping you with spiritual weapons for your own battles, leaving you with a stronger faith, ready to fight for the promises He has for your life.

It's a personal choice to trust, to obey, and to use God's Word as the sword in the battle against the enemy. Satan will try to steal God's truth from your heart, mind, body, and spirit—but we are called to invite God into our struggles for solutions not just to describe our troubles to Him.

In a world that constantly slights Jesus, I believe we were made for this time, as Esther 4:14b reminds us: *"Yet who knows whether you have come to the kingdom for such a time as this?"*

My prayer is for others to never give up, no matter what the world or the experts say. Keep your faith strong. Believe in miracles. And know this: God did not cause your pain, loss, or hardship, but He will be the one to

INTRODUCTION

carry you through it. Be unwavering in knowing that God's love is limitless and that He can do for anyone, regardless of their circumstances. He is the solution, not the cause, through every bad situation, providing the things that we cannot do for ourselves to get through it all.

May these words heal your hurt, empower your weak spots, strengthen your faith, and fill your heart with hope and peace as you face the toughest circumstances. May you leave these pages knowing that His power is real, as is His promise of Heaven—all available to you.

CHAPTER 1
DOING LIFE

"Moreover whom He predestined, these He also called; whom He called, these He also justified; and whom He justified, these He also glorified."
—Romans 8:30

My son, Louis Shane Hadley, was born on January 5, 1992, in Spearfish, South Dakota, into a ranching and rodeo family. He was fortunate to grow up on a beautiful ranch in northeast Wyoming, nestled at the edge of the Black Hills, one of the most picturesque and historically rich regions Wyoming has to offer. Unlike the expansive wilderness of Yellowstone or the towering peaks of Jackson Hole, the Black Hills are more accessible. They offer an inviting combination of pine forests and attainable summits, perfect for both snow skiing in the winter and water skiing in the summer. From the rolling, sage-covered pastures, you can even catch a glimpse of the nation's first national monument, Devils Tower, which stands as a marvel to travelers from all over the world.

The SY Ranch, where our family lived and worked, spans 40,000 acres of God's glory, ideal for a working cattle operation. Here, we cared for 350 mother cows and ran between 1,500 to 1,750 head of yearling cattle annually because of Jim's expert stewardship. The ranch was so beautiful and efficient that a banker, who had seen ranches from one end of the country to the other, considered it one of the top two he'd ever encountered.

The meaning of the name Shane from Irish origin is "God is gracious." In Hebrew, it means "beautiful." Shane and his sister, Shiloh, shared this real working cowboy life. Shane, the youngest of the two, often said he didn't have a mom and a sister—he had two moms. Despite their sibling differences, Shane and Shiloh shared a bond that was special. They were blessed to grow up living the true cowboy life: roping, driving, and dragging cattle to the branding fire. They helped care for newborn calves during spring snowstorms, bottle-feeding those that had lost their mothers or for being a twin from a cow that didn't have enough milk for two.

Shane and Shiloh spent countless hours riding the vast Wyoming landscape, sometimes trailing 700 yearlings across the open range. Even before they were out of elementary school, they could be trusted to help move and control the herd. They'd often arrive late to school because they had been busy helping gather cattle down off a half-mile hill, bringing them into the corral. Afterward, their grandmother would drive them to school, their horses tied up in the barn.

On a working cow ranch, whether you're a cowboy or a cowgirl, the work is the same. Shane and Shiloh worked right alongside the grown-ups, doing everything from pushing cattle to tending to the daily chores that were crucial to the operation. I remember Shane, so young, with his imaginary friend, "Uncle Shane," who, in Shane's eyes, had already done everything he wanted to do. It was a source of endless amusement for us. Shane would talk to him out loud while riding, often getting so caught up in conversation that we had to call out to him, "Shane, quit talking and get up here!" And then he'd chime in with what he and Uncle Shane had been discussing, always so smart and so funny.

Watching Shane grow up in that environment, I couldn't help but marvel at how the ranch and the cowboy way of life shaped him. With adult jobs came adult responsibility. Excuses were not accepted. There were no clocks to look at to say time's up with work. You stay hooked until the last cow's moved or the last job's done. Cows could care less how old you are, or what gender. Discrimination is a human thing. Right's right, wrong's wrong, you do right by others, and you treat others kindly. It's a gentleman's cowboy way to stand up for those who can't take it for themselves. I don't think it can be taught any other way except caring for animals trying to live in the harshest conditions.

That, in itself, with a family that comes from a rodeo background as well as ranch cowboying, was definitely the thing that Shane did at a young age that prepared him for a "no-excuses" future. Shane was expected to not only help, but his dad and I wanted to equip him with the confidence to know by having those responsibilities that we respected his ability enough to provide good help. It's a beautiful thing to set up others to build confidence in what can be possible if you simply believe in them and let them try. All kids raised on a farm or ranch have the opportunity to appreciate what God has given us, not only in provision and resources but also in the talent to know how to care best for them.

Shiloh and Shane had the city cousins, as they called themselves, come to the ranch on so many different occasions. We ran them in a herd most holidays and every summer. Those children in Shane's life were older, and he always was the happy little kid wanting to be part of everything, always wanting to make everyone laugh. They all enjoyed the vastness that we so often take for granted and ran about it in glee. They learned to brand and rope and ride along with their ranch cousins. Shane and Shiloh were grateful to be a part of those older cousins' every adventure and would learn all the city activities, joking about things like bicycles, skateboards, and swim lessons. Shane was the youngest of the six, so he idolized everything they did. And the only time he really got to talk was at the dinner table when they were eating. He would hold court with his older cousins, and they would just listen as they ate. He has always been the funniest one, trying to make everybody laugh.

Shane had little to no shame. He would trip and fall in front of the whole gymnasium, trying to make the wave happen and just get up and laugh and go on with it. He notices people around him. He always has, since he was little. He wants to help. He wants to be in the mix of things. He was the kid who was always selfless. The young man that some dads and moms wanted their daughters to marry. When Shane was in college, the rodeo team would have different issues—someone with a flat tire, the coach needing someone to take ropes off for the ropers, even though he probably was just there for steer wrestling at the time. Shane was always the one to help, and in our family, he became "Hey Somebody" because, inevitably, if we needed something, we would go, "Hey, somebody needs to do that." And I would turn and say, "Hey Somebody, hey Shane," because he was bigger than life and capable of anything as a grown young man. So strong and willing.

When he was younger, in grade school, there was a kid being bullied, and Shane took it upon himself to stick up for the kid that was being bullied. Unfortunately, not stopping there, he decided to also rub the other child's face in the dirt. Needless to say, he got in trouble, too, trying to do the right thing, but it's kind of how the cowboy way has been taught. If you don't respect your elders, then you will respect your *betters*.

Shane was so selfless that Shiloh, in high school and college, struggled with sports knee injuries four different times and constantly battled back to get back on the court or back on her horse. To help her, Shane would pick up the slack. He would saddle all the horses. He would get them warmed up, bring the horse to the fence where Shiloh would crawl onto the saddle, go rope her calf in pain, and when the run was completed, take the horse so she could continue to recover. Shane would do the chores, feedings, and tend to everything else. On mornings before school, Shane—though he was now a junior in high school—would get the car, shovel snow, fill it up if needed, pull it up to the gate, and watch his sister come running out. He would then politely move to the passenger side and let her drive them to school. He was okay with it. He didn't care. He was just glad to be a blessing all the time and did it even into his adult life and on through injury, his own injuries. Today, he's still helping.

He played football from the fourth grade, which allowed him to thrive in high school. Shane and his three closest friends started in little league football, playing together all through junior high and high school, and they played tough. Shane's dad coached them, and other dads volunteered during the formative years. Everyone's favorite memory from those early days was when the boys were in fourth grade, and Jim gave some coaching advice to one of the more timid players on the team. He said, "If you aren't going to block 'em, fall down in front of them so they at least have to jump over you." That line still cracks us up. All of those boys were the band of brothers heading into high school, and being from a small school, they were the boys often found in the royalty court or homecoming lineup. They were the ones the girls teased and flirted with, and the ones who made everyone laugh.

Their work ethic and team mentality to give selflessly was why he started varsity football all four years of high school. We had a huge offensive line when Shane was a freshman, but because Shane could block and was efficient at it, he was our center. Our offensive line was shaped like a "V" because of our big lineman and smaller center. We were so proud that he could play both sides of the ball, but defense was his forte. In the final years of high school, Shane was number one in defensive stats in the whole state of Wyoming, all divisions, until the playoffs. Shane led in all defensive categories except for interceptions for the entire state and in all divisions until the other teams went into the playoffs.

Unfortunately, our team wasn't as successful in those years. It takes the entire team, and we needed all players to have as much heart and try as Shane. He went on to Chadron to play football in college, but he gave up a lot of pounds. As much as he had heart, he was 5'11" and weighed 185 pounds as a senior. He equates his shortness to his mother's 5'4" stature. But even as he bulked up to 203 pounds, he was still the smallest guy on the team next to the kicker. Needless to say, his heart got a little injured, along with his shoulder injury, and that ended his football career.

Prior to that, in the pursuit of always trying to be funny, Shane slid by with mischievous acts that bordered on the need for reproof from faculty members because he was smart and his grades were good. When he was a kid, we would play trivia, especially anything to do with the Disney movies at that time. During Disney trivia, all the older kids would just give up because they couldn't keep up with Shane's recall of all of the minute details in those movies. He did the same with National Geographic facts about animals and places at a really early age. His schoolwork was no different. He could just read it once or absorb it in class. He didn't always have to bring a book home, and he made the honor roll. So he was a scholar athlete who was fun to be around and thoughtful of others. To watch him grow into a man who continued doing that, living up to his name of "Hey Somebody Hadley," was rewarding for every generation he touched.

Despite not living in a football town as one might witness in Texas, he really truly was a football champ to us. My favorite memory performance was from the Shrine Bowl with players from the North and the South of the entire state of Wyoming. Shane made the team for the North, but the coach for his position was the dad to the player starting in his defensive position. Shane had not seen game time, and we were deep into the fourth quarter. The South was within our 10-yard line with four downs in an attempt to score. Being the vocal football mom that I am, I was yelling to put in number 51. Much to my delight, out went Shane. Not only was he the defensive tackle and the first to make a stop on every play during the first three downs, but on the fourth down, he also tipped the pass—preventing the opposing team from scoring and allowing us to recover the ball. He stayed in the game as they marched down the field, and when it mattered most, Shane, playing as the center, snapped the ball for the game-winning field goal. The team scored, securing the victory for the North!

Yet, just as man makes his plans, the Lord directs his steps. Because God is so good and He blessed Shane with talent, he moved on to rodeo with his sister down at Tarleton State University in Stephenville, Texas, after his football injury. He got a rodeo scholarship, steer wrestled, team roped, and calf roped when he came down to Texas, thus opening a new door of hope after finishing his high school rodeo time as an alternate and runner-up to qualifying nationally in steer wrestling. He roped in his younger years, but as a football player, it's easy to see how the two sports connect on levels of grit, brute force, and determination. Both require a formidable "let's get it on" mentality, a dismissal of danger, and, most assuredly, an adrenaline rush.

The Powers and Hadley families come from a family lineage of rodeo. Shane's maternal grandfather was a founding turtle member of the Rodeo Cowboys Association, which is now known as the PRCA, the Professional Rodeo Cowboys Association. Research says that more than 30 different rodeo organizations are recognized, and over 15 other related sports stem from rodeo. There are thousands of rodeos held worldwide each year. They were around as early as the 1820s when there was a competition between the cowboys and vaqueros from the U.S. and Mexico. The competition started based on the jobs caring for the cattle on ranches. July 4, 1883, in Pecos, Texas, the town in which my father, Louis Powers, was inducted to their Rodeo Hall of Fame, is where an argument between Travis Windham, a cattle driver, and Morg Livingston, an accomplished cattle roper led to what the world refers to the "world's first public cowboy contest." Now, there are nine major professional events in rodeo, although more events exist. There are two major categories: timed events and rough stock events. The performance of rodeo revitalizes the spirit of the Old West of a "man-animal" opposition, showing the conflict between the wild and the tame.

Jim, Shane's dad, is a Mountain States champion calf roper and gold card holder in the Professional Rodeo Cowboys Association. I myself am a Women's National Finals Rodeo qualifier in the team roping for the Women's Professional Rodeo Association four times, and I have been inducted into the All Cowboy and Arena Champions Hall of Fame and into the Texas Rodeo Cowboy Hall of Fame. We felt that the kids were more than likely going to compete in rodeo as a direct result of the influence of our whole family from both sides. It is wonderful to see that they embraced it and loved it as much as we do because the lessons in life that you learn through rodeo cannot be taught in any other sport. You have to go beyond yourself, and in the timed events of rodeo, care for and depend on an animal for your success, and you absolutely depend on other animals that you don't have control of in both the bucking rough stock events and the timed events. There is much at play, and trust is key, as is trusting in the Lord to be faithful to the promises in His Word.

LOOK UP

The "left wanting" steer wrestling alternate position to go to nationals was another driving factor. Shane, having always competed and won in team roping and calf roping, loved the sport as a whole, yet steer wrestling got him particularly excited. Steer wrestling, historically, was not a part of ranch life. The event originated in the 1890s and is claimed to have been started by a Black cowboy named Bill Pickett, a wild-west show performer. Some stories claim that he developed the idea after he observed how cattle dogs worked with unruly animals.

Steer wrestling, also known as bulldogging, is an event that involves two normally 1,200-pound horses with two cowboys mounted on them and one 600 to 750-pound steer in between them. The mounted rider on the steer's right will chase the steer simultaneously to serve as a blocker to keep the steer running straight as the rider mounted on the left chases, drops from the horse to the steer, and then wrestles the steer to the ground by grabbing its horns and pulling it off balance so that it falls to the ground. The event carries a high risk of injury to the cowboy.

We take for granted how dangerous rodeo and being horseback truly is because it's how we grew up; it was our lifestyle and how we made our living, putting beef on the table for America. Still, we don't realize how dangerous it can be. Yet, we were so sad about his shoulder injury but quietly thankful for the knocking helmets on the field, the physics of that being over, and that new adventures could await.

So unfortunately, injury brought a blessing as we could see it. In Texas, he was awarded a college rodeo scholarship—steer wrestling, calf roping, and team roping. It was natural. Rodeo gives you something that no other sport does—the responsibility of your animals. You don't rely on anybody but yourself in most of the events besides the animals that you're competing with. The success that is most rewarded is hard work, and I feel the sport closely exemplifies sportsmanship. People help each other, loan their horses, give their animals a push, or haze the steer for them while they're winning the steer wrestling or roping themselves. It's a beautiful, selfless way to compete when you rodeo. Ranching is no different in the fact that you, as a cowboy, put yourself above those animals to keep them alive in conditions on the ranch—relentless care that helps the animals so that they perform to the best of their ability.

You learn selflessness through that care, and that's what comes to mind when you hear the word "cowboy." Then you have the "Code of the West," a set of principles rooted in the good Lord's guidance on what's right and wrong, rephrased by cowboys and called the Code of the West. These spoken Scriptures guide our lives and help us maintain a strong relationship with God. We don't waver. Our *yes* is our *yes*. Our *no* is our *no*. And with that, God can do a lot.

Many times, our words limit what is available to us. If you first don't believe something can happen and speak the truth of what you believe, then, to me, God stands on the sidelines, handcuffed by what you, yourself, haven't conceived it to be. When Scripture says, "Speak things that be not as they may," it means you can release all the help from God and heaven above by repeating the promise in Scripture with a simple prayer of thanksgiving to God for what you hope to happen as if it has happened already. Thank the Lord beforehand for the things in His will you hope to happen—health, rain, healing, safe travel, reconciliation, restoration, provision, and salvation through His Son, Jesus Christ. As cowboys, coupled with belief and faith, there's no backup for us. When you need somebody to rely on, you don't have to wonder if they're going to waver, not to mention be moved, when there is hardship or opposition. When you choose to believe in God, you don't make Him prove it to you. You truly trust and obey the Word—all in on heavenly things navigating the earthly. The cowboys I grew up admiring won't waver. We love that. I feel Shane has embodied that and carried that in his spirit even at a young age. He had a job here and there, just constantly being a blessing. Accountable.

Shockingly, Jim and I were basically forced off the family ranch after decades of Jim's loyalty to his family; it was a pretty devastating blow. It wasn't because of job performance, as the profit margins can easily show annually. As a duly and twice elected county commissioner with eight years of service to the county, the full-time load of all ranch operations, and being an excellent steward of the land, he proved his capabilities. His responsibilities consisted of moving, working, doctoring, and branding all the cattle, baling, stacking, or purchasing the hay, monitoring all pasture usage, and fencing the entire 40,000 acres of miles of requirement.

Jim was the brains of hedging and figuring futures of the cattle in the market; he was the bookkeeper of said assets and liabilities without much oversight—all for a low enough wage that we depended on the humble assets brought in from serving civically. All the while, being frugal with not only the ranch's best interests but those of the county as well, earning Jim the nickname of "Dr. No" with fellow county officials, for if it was a want, the answer was no, and if it was a need, it was made to be justified.

Performance was not in question, but nevertheless, we followed our kids to Texas, where I grew up, as we no longer had a job, a vehicle, our home, nothing. It was pretty brutal. Shane and Shiloh were in school, and we'd been asked to leave the ranch; we were literally homeless and without a vehicle. We had horses everywhere. We had rodeo people taking us in. We had my childhood Texas friends rescuing us—irreplaceable help and creativity in storing what we hauled from Texas to Wyoming, aptly named Operation Wyoming Rescue, we all joke about a decade later. So many people stepped up and helped in ways that there's no way we could ever repay or have enough time in this book to name in that mission in fear of leaving someone out.

In Texas, it was just us, no vengeful family members, passive or participatory, stopping us from surviving. Our kids took care of us while earning their college degrees. We watched them walk across the stage for business and teaching degrees with no blood family present besides ourselves.

The one person I will name is Clarice Hedeman, the surrogate mom/grandmother and matriarch, who stepped up like she has all of my life, along with her two awesome daughters, Cheryl and Jane. In fact, had it not been for Jane I wouldn't be here a decade later writing these words. Her extensive ER and almost half a century of nursing are what made a life-saving difference in the first 10 days of my cancer battle. When Jane asks you to be tough, she is the real cowgirl deal, and she means it, as does Cheryl and the ones they have raised where tough is expected.

In Shiloh and Shane's formative years, we gave them no choice and made no promises of ranch payment, yet they willingly gave us their childhood, continuing to care for the needs of the ranch and our family. For that, their dad and I will remain not only deeply grateful but also incredibly proud.

During that time, the family had decided that Jim and my services were no longer needed on the ranch, as Jim was having undiagnosed health issues and I, shortly after being diagnosed with stage 3 ovarian cancer, left us in need. Jim had worked on his family's ranch for over 60 years. Without going into further detail—and as we try to make sense of it ourselves—if you look up the symptoms of narcissistic behavior, you'll see that we have experienced some of the consequences and hardships that come with it.

Shane was told to his face by his only living paternal grandparent that Shiloh was his favorite, and it set Shane up to not look to other hurting humans for the things that you can do for yourself or the things they themselves are not capable of doing. The choice was independence or insecurity sprinkled with misplaced approval seeking. I am glad the Holy Spirit inside of Him allowed Shane to believe what God says, that His love is equal for all. Independently loved by God, equal to all, inferior to none. Put your faith in the one from which love comes and let it flow through to those around you. Be like Shane and Shiloh. They were real cowboy help, and no one can take those memories, whether their contributions were noticed and deemed worthy or not.

When Shane was rodeoing in college, he was roommates with different ones and sometimes with his sister, and he was constantly the one that would pick up the rent if anything was short on another one's end, as well as doing the chores that others didn't want to do. After my diagnosis of cancer, instead of going to finally live his dream to have the opportunity to go rodeo, Shane was sleeping on the concrete floor at man camp on his birthday to start a new job in the oil field to make enough money to sustain us all and still have some left for his fees to compete when able.

Shane had a major job, helping his parents get into a home so they didn't have to pay rent any longer and they could get some equity going. Because of Shane's job, he helped us sign the note—while working 17 to 18 hours a day at Mitchell Pipe, trying to get practice after hours, running here and there on the weekends, and trying to rodeo, getting back at 3 a.m. before work the next morning. As if things weren't trying enough, Jim had officially been identified as having the symptoms of Parkinson's, and I was in a major battle with ovarian cancer.

But guess what? Shane was still "Hey Somebody" Shane. But don't think, as his mom, I wasn't aware of the streak of ornery in the boy. Unlike his sister, whose face said, "I'm so lying, and I'm about to just spill the beans on the whole truth!" Shane could tell you an untruth so convincingly that you'd believe it, only to burst into a belly laugh once he knew he had you fooled. He was definitely the son being interrogated by his mom about the previous night's adventures: "Where did you go?"

"Nowhere."

"Who did you see?"

"No one."

"What did you do?"

"Nothing."

Your secrets were always safe with him.

Of all the opposition and trials in life that every person goes through, I know none of us want to speak ill of family, but to provide the facts of the matter so as not to diminish what God has done and continues to do. If you listen to the story and what our family has overcome, you realize that it takes no certain or particular human to help you get through the most arduous and hard times of your life because God will provide the humans that want to be the hands and feet. And when we step up to that, we're being the blessing that we're called to be. And that's what I feel Shane has always tried to embody by helping those who need it. Shane was the one who would pick up some day work so he'd have the extra cash and wouldn't have to rely on anybody else. It is a beautiful thing to see what God calls us all to do. We're blessed to be a blessing. When others believed to be our greatest support fell short, we knew to look to our Godly, Heavenly Father, who can fulfill the promises of heaven and help give us the right choices to make and the strength to endure what other humans cannot provide.

Our story is one sad one to tell, as we sometimes laugh that we're kind of like a sad country song, except they did everything but kick our dog and steal our Bible. Yet we still stand here to tell you, don't lose hope. That never stopped any of us. We just kept moving on and looking up.

CHAPTER 2
LET'S RODEO! KINDA...

"Not that I have already attained, or am already perfected; but I press on, that I may lay hold of that for which Christ Jesus has also laid hold of me. Brethren, I do not count myself to have apprehended; but one thing I do, forgetting those things which are behind and reaching forward to those things which are ahead, I press toward the goal for the prize of the upward call of God in Christ Jesus."
—Philippians 3:12-14

As Shane was working hard over in the Midland, Texas area several hours away from us in Stephenville, he would come home and take care of us, but, at this point, Jim had been misdiagnosed. They had him on medication for familial tremors, as his Parkinson's had not yet been identified. I was in the middle of cancer treatment, a series of 24 infusions of chemotherapy every three weeks. Shane knew we needed help with the basic day-to-day tasks, so he found a job in Stephenville and moved in to help take care of us.

His absence was felt when he left West Texas. On the rigs, he was the guy who everyone couldn't help but like, no matter what, and he brought the same spirit with him to Stephenville, too. I still meet people who remember Shane as such a joy, complimenting me on the young man that he is—I couldn't have been more proud. Yet, while he was there taking care of us, he hadn't relinquished his hope of competing professionally. He won here and there but was constantly having to find a horse to ride. Shane was recovering from an injury, his horse had been crippled, and even after healing, the horse still needed an extra step. Despite the obstacles, Shane managed to qualify, gain, earn, and fill his permit in the Professional Rodeo Cowboys Association in steer wrestling to earn his professional card. It wasn't surprising that Shane's pro start came while we were still on the ranch. Just a few dollars shy of filling his permit to qualify for his professional card, he and Jim had been up all night fighting fires to save the pastures, timber, fences, and animals. Yet, after that sleepless night, Shane won his first ProRodeo in steer wrestling, with his dad hazing the steer for him. Energized from the win, Shane drove back to the ranch while Jim slept, and they returned to the fire, which was still not fully contained. Selfless.

After working hard to gain his permit after college, he decided to compete in what rodeos he could. Soon, Shane decided that he wanted to pro rodeo. He qualified for the Texas Circuit Finals Top 12 and ended up second in the circuit. The circuit system for the Professional Rodeo Cowboys Association is highly competitive in North America, with 650 events held annually across the nation. The country is divided into 12 geographical regions. Each PRCA member designates his home circuit and must compete in at least 15 rodeos within that circuit to qualify for the circuit finals. He was looking forward to trying to win enough to compete full-time since we were starting to get on our feet despite our ailments and injuries and things we were battling. Shane had been operating as usual: working out, caring for us, practicing when he could, and giving the rest of his time to Mitchell Pipe. He struggled with the idea of leaving, and he started putting pressure on the next few rodeos he went to.

Shane and Shiloh knew how to be accountable from the hard work and the dedication that they put into the ranch as children. I bristled at the calls from others—unknowing taunts about their loved ones heading to a rodeo or doing this or that. I could only wish them well while yearning for my son to have the same unhindered path. My heart would break a little each time, wishing he had spent the week in the practice pen instead of at man camp. It was hard to watch Shane sacrifice his best interests for someone else.

We have been taught that God is no respecter of persons; He loves us all equally. I believe in the Scripture and the promise that He will "reward those who diligently seek Him." During the time Shane was at man camp, he attended a small, old church. One day, a lady there asked him, "Would you like to be baptized today?" Shane called us and said, "I got baptized today."

I replied, "You did what?"

He said, "Yeah, I just felt like I needed to do it again. They dunked me this time."

At the end of their primary school years when Shiloh and Shane were baptized as children in the Methodist church, the pastor had returned from Israel with water from the River Jordan, where Jesus was baptized, and that water was sprinkled over them. The Bible tells us that professing Christ is the most important choice anyone can make, and we felt so blessed that Shane wanted to reaffirm that decision. It was yet another example of what set Shane apart from his peers at the time.

We couldn't be more proud of the way he was taking care of us, striving to do the right things, and still pursuing his dream of rodeoing after college and reaching the professional level. Practice wasn't nearby—it was an hour and a half drive each way. After a full day of driving around delivering pipe, he would make the trip, only to drive back, grab a shower, get a few hours of rest, and wake up to do it all over again.

It took immense effort to find time to work out, stay in physical shape, and practice to remain sharp for professional competition—all while giving one hundred percent effort to the people who provided his paycheck each month. That alone was a full-time job, not to mention all the help we needed here and there. Yet, he handled it all with grace, humor, punctuality, and consistency, continuing to be the blessing he had been since he was little.

Because of his high school injuries, he faced setbacks, underwent rehab, and worked hard to address issues that had hindered his performance in the past. In that sense, he is no different from any contestant out there striving to overcome challenges and beat the odds.

You can prepare and do your best, but ultimately, in many instances, the draw determines your success from one event to another, so you have to pull some good ones to win. Consistently, the numbers speak for themselves. Shane's odds were just as hard as everybody else's out there—he had extra responsibilities. Still, he didn't let that stop him from achieving what he did and winning the rodeos that helped him qualify for the Texas Circuit Finals in the Top 12. Yet, that second position for the Texas Circuit didn't provide a straight shot to success. He was still working long hours as a delivery driver, constantly challenged by things beyond his control—schedules, timing, and others' needs. Life dictated his choices more than selfish desire. Having thoughts like: *Shane, if you don't make this jackpot, you don't get to go here.* Therefore, he had to be deliberate with his choice to still be fair to his position in the company, which often forced which rodeos he would get to use his time off to attend.

He worked longer shifts earlier in the week, so he had the ability to leave earlier at week's end to go to the rodeos on the weekend. He was in the gym, 205 pounds, four percent body fat, and giving it his all because football taught him how to nutritionally and physically prepare. Nothing is wasted in your life in the world of sport. I've seen it pay for college educations for many of our family members, and it was no different with Shane and Shiloh. Their scholarships provided them with degrees. His Tarleton degree is in business. It's truly amazing how much self-discipline can come from the sport of rodeo, and I think every successful athlete knows how to use it to propel them where others aren't willing to go. We hoped that Shane was applying it in his life while also finding time to practice and horses to ride.

While he was managing all of this, he would drive me to my infusions if needed. Often, I would simply drive myself, meeting Jim afterward to rope—or, if not after, I would go rope *before* chemotherapy, refusing to give in to sickness. Planning to do the things you love is one of the best ways to get through the things you don't love. For me, that meant roping. I still like to get on horseback with the challenge of catching a bovine.

As Jim's health improved and he was placed on the right medication, he was able to function better. This allowed Shane to focus more on his own goals without being sidetracked by caregiving responsibilities. That didn't stop his constant checking in to make sure all our needs were met, but it gave him the ability to press forward, working even harder toward his dreams.

To qualify for the Fort Worth Rodeo—where he once won the first round—it was necessary to win some of the smaller rodeos first. He put a lot of emphasis on those qualifying events, which meant he could no longer rely solely on the animal he had. Instead, he had to push beyond what was available to him, sometimes forcing things to happen. And therein lay the heightened risk.

We watched this young man work tirelessly, refusing to leave any room for excuses when it came to his own success. He put in the effort. He showed up. And it was beautiful to witness how everything came together —revealing just how deeply he cared for everyone around him.

As we saw our son continue to grow into a beautiful man, the pattern was consistent. He cared for others, and he put action—not words— behind it. And as he continued to endure the challenges that proved to make it difficult for him, he would make it work. So, we considered Shane ready for battle. Any time there was a loss or unsuccessfulness in the arena, the mentality was simply, *Look up. You're already blessed. You're there.* We've lost many, so go and do it for those who aren't here or able, as well as for yourself. We all have hardships, but then we are presented with a choice. We can either be powerful, or we can be pitiful—but we can't be both. So when you choose to be powerful, you choose to be solution-minded. You choose to do the next right thing. You choose to say, *Well, what is the solution to the hardship? What makes it better?* And as I watched Shane refine himself, it's not unlike when you refine silver and gold. Once it goes through the fire, it takes out all the impurities and just leaves the good things.

When you do everything that you do unto the Lord, it doesn't matter if you are cowboying, if you're scrubbing floors, or if you're the CEO. You do your work in excellence unto Him, and you can take pride and glory in whatever you're doing. No man or no human can take away the self-fulfillment of living up to God's expectations instead of their own.

When you are on horseback, that animal doesn't care if you're a cowboy or cowgirl, and they don't care what age you are. There was a saying I saw once that said, "Some of Wyoming's best cowboys are cowgirls," and it's true. There was a lot of responsibility on both Shane and Shiloh as children, and they just took it in stride and learned the work ethic that you learn growing up on a ranch or a farm, where the whole nation is dependent on you making sure you get those cows to market and food on the table for America.

When the kids were still young, Shiloh was the bigger sister in every sense of the word, at least a head taller. Bigger than Shane for a while, towering over him and tough. She was raised around boys and grown men, and to this day, if I had to pick somebody in the mix to get something done, I'd pick Shiloh. The boys are a great help. But there's a saying, "If you have one boy, you have a whole boy. If you have two boys, you have half a boy. And, if you have three boys, you have no boy at all!" Shiloh was my best help.

Before Shane had matured, a slight lesson in physics was learned while wrangling the horses. The two of them were coming from the corral they had put the horses in. You could tell they were arguing about something from my view from the kitchen window. I saw Shane push Shiloh from behind and pop her head back. She turned around and punched him right in the mouth. *Wham!* I ran out there and I told her, as a woman, if the rule stands that a man can not hit a woman, then a woman can't hit a man.

Period. She was reprimanded and reminded of that lesson, no matter if she could pull it off. I then turned to Shane and informed him that no matter how tough he thought he was, he had better learn. She had twice the reach on him, so he'd better watch himself.

He grew up just laughing at her later when they got older, and he could hold her away at his arm's length. It's all giggling fun as far as childhood memories go, and at that time, I remember riding along and listening to Shane say that his teeth hurt. I said, "Well, you shouldn't have taken your sister on, son. Get up here, ride your horse, you will be alright. We have to move these cows." Life as they knew it didn't give up too much sympathy. It was a tough, "rub some dirt on it" environment, but a blessed life that these kids got to live.

Growing up in West Texas, if it wasn't poking, biting, or stinging, then you weren't in the pastures of West Texas! We are a product of our surroundings. Imagine my delight at the lushness of Wyoming spring and summers. Winters, of course, had the longest run, and fall got shorter, as did spring. The kids, like myself, didn't know any better, and they stepped up to the plate. I feel like that's why Shane had such a work ethic. He didn't ask us for a single dime when he went to college. He paid for his own truck, which we continued to use after they asked us to leave the ranch. That's how we survived.

Those trials prune off the things that keep you from being all that God calls you to be. The excellence that you seek just being a child in His image. That drive is more focused and more appreciated and more understood of what your purpose is when you go through the trials, and you find out what really is important in all of this. What is the priority? First, glorify God in everything, and the rest will follow or not matter. Be better than you were the day before. When you stay real with yourself through the hardships of it, you can overcome them. You won't get stuck in them.

I watched Shane navigate anything that was difficult—challenges taught him how to do that, fight through it, and be resilient, the cowboy way—no giving up, no backing out, no quitting. Then and only then will you be able to put those cowboy euphemisms into practice. They're not just little sayings. You get to live it. It's a true and pure—put up or shut up kind of attitude. The stoic old silent cowboys don't use words, they just use their actions. They let their good work show through their deeds. They let their good work show their heart and their attitude. They won't get mushy about it, and they won't give themselves much credit, if any, for it. You're just expected to do what's right.

We have several cowboy friends, Rob Smets being the main one, along with Shane and for many of us, the mantra is: "Do what's right because it's right." There's no fanfare or "atta boys" for doing what's right because it's simply expected. When viewed through the lens of doing what's right because it's right, it helps you avoid getting caught up in the challenges coming against you—the negative distractions and discouragements that can paralyze you. These things don't bring life to the solution or align with God's will, so they don't deserve our attention. Instead, the focus should be on what we can do to make things better. *What's the next right step we can take? How can we improve?* We are blessed to be a blessing. Seek wisdom from above to navigate life while helping yourself and those around you.

There was more in store for Shane than being a rodeo star, and we all had to look up to see God's promises and His excellence.

CHAPTER 3
YOU THINK YOU'RE GOOD, BUT BE BETTER

"Be anxious for nothing, but in everything by prayer and supplication, with thanksgiving, let your requests be made known to God; and the peace of God, which surpasses all understanding, will guard your hearts and minds through Christ Jesus."
–Philippians 4:6-8

Whether working cattle in modern times or during the massive drives of the past, cowboys don't get to quit. You can't stop just because things are tough or the conditions are arduous. Shane carried that same grit from birth, always riding on. He graduated from college with a business degree from Tarleton and worked tirelessly to help us secure a home, find jobs, and pay for everything.

He also did horse bodywork on the side, manipulating not just like a chiropractor but releasing the muscles and tendons that pull the bones out of proper alignment. His natural talent produced results, providing some horses with much-needed relief—you could see the change in them. It was beautiful work. He learned this skill and was paid by people to help their horses. Shane also helped catch and work the wild game raised by our friends Liz and Casey McGlaun. I have been friends with Casey since our junior rodeo days, and Liz and I lived in Fort Worth at the same time after college. Precious friends and even more special people. I remember him working with mouflon sheep (wild ancestors of domestic sheep), wild aoudad (Barbary sheep, native to North Africa), and other wild game for the McGlauns, always lending a hand. Every day, Shane Hadley hit the ground running.

He was working, he was working out, he was practicing, he was earning his money, and he wasn't asking people for anything except practice because he was too busy giving to everybody. So the morning of May 12th, 2018, was no different. He'd gone, put a full day at Mitchell Pipe, and came home through the door at a tornado's pace, changing into cowboy clothes and official PRCA attire, before driving us to Mineral Wells, where we were meeting up with Liz and Casey for dinner, and heading to the arena. He was all business, and this particular rodeo was very important to him. He felt he strongly needed to win this rodeo to get into the bigger ones, and to make enough money to not leave everybody in financial hardship—always thinking of others before himself. But the pressure, the emphasis that was put on that run was just blind determination. Perhaps Shane had stepped out of allowing God to guide him through the journey and timing needed to stay on course. Maybe he tried to force things and take control into his own hands, as the moments that unfolded afterward seemed destined not to deviate from this path.

I felt weird. Indescribably so. I felt like we needed to hurry and let him get there. I kept feeling this, like, *go ahead, baby, get to the arena.* After we finished dinner with Liz and Casey, we went to the arena and drove to the back, where the trailers were parked and the steer wrestlers were getting ready. Shane was stretching to get on Baby Colt, the horse he was riding that night that belonged to Blake Doyle. Sam Williams was going to haze. Shane was just really serious, so I didn't want to stick around and make him make small talk. I remember ushering us to the arena and getting to a seat in the stands right next to the arena fence. The bulldogging started; Shane was farther down in the contestant list for that night. The cattle were not that great.

Later, it was rumored that, in the preceding weeks, the cattle had been "broken in" using motorcycles instead of horses. This meant they were repeatedly released from the box and shown the location of the arena's back-end let-out gate without horses on either side if that was the case. Therefore they had not been prepared in the way in which the event is performed. This is a huge no-no in the world of true professional preparation of timed event cattle.

I don't mean to be critical of our rodeo family. We know that sometimes, as far as timed event cattle goes, they are hard to find and even harder to get nice, or even set. They do try, but we understand they don't get recognition for their timed event cattle. There are a lot of awards for how good their rough stock animals are; the timed event of the arena is hard work and not the glamorous part of stock contracting. I don't know how the cattle were broken in that arena, but none of them were running straight, and they weren't giving the boys a good chance to make a run at all.

In the rough stock world, if the animal doesn't perform to a decent amount of competitiveness then contestants get a re-ride. There's no such thing in the timed events of rodeo. There's no reruns. You get a bad draw? *Tough luck. Thanks for coming. Try again at the next one.* It's the luck of the draw. And so, when these steers were going left and right and stopping, and nobody was getting a time, the clown in the arena was trying to be funny and entertain the crowd and said, "Well, man, if they don't get a time pretty soon, I'm going to have to run one."

But guess whose turn it was: Mr. Determination. Mr. "I'm going to get it done." Before he even nodded his head, I saw Shane's determination to get a time. In an event where the 600-plus pound steer runs anywhere from 17-25 miles per hour, and a 1500-pound quarter horse and rider running 30 mph, it makes for some serious force in play. Shane nodded his head, and the steer went hard left. In steer wrestling, that's the most dangerous move a steer can make on a cowboy. Instead of pulling his horse up, Shane just kept riding. He was trying to get around that steer and get a time. He was forcing it. The steer never weakened, but neither did Shane. He had tried to ride and get around him, but when the steer suddenly turned, the steer's hind end tripped the horse. It caused his horse to "t-bone" the steer with all that physics of speed and pounds in play.

When it tripped his horse, he never dropped his hands from the reins or the saddle horn, and it sent Shane's head first, and the horse rolled over the top of him. After Shane went out of sight and came out from underneath the horse, right at that moment, I knew he was really hurt. He landed at my feet with one eye open and one eye shut. Hysterical, I jumped over the arena fence down 10 or 12 feet to the arena floor, and I was the first one to him. My phone in hand still recording, you hear my screams in the video that, somehow, was saved in the chaos.

At the time, I thought it was the rodeo clown trying to calm me down, but another kind cowboy later told me he had. I wasn't helping matters—in hindsight, I was probably terrorizing everyone in the stands. The EMTs were moving at a snail's pace to get to Shane. I knew it was bad; it didn't take a rocket scientist to see that if one eye was open and the other was shut, there was a serious problem.

When they finally got into the arena to take Shane to the ambulance, people caring for him seemed to be in shock. Incidents like this didn't happen often, but when they did, they were serious. The ambulance crew was visibly shaken, saying things like, "At least the heart's okay." Meanwhile, I was screaming at them to do something because it was clear they weren't acting fast enough.

At that moment, a firefighter from Mineral Wells named Chris Brooks, our little angel, heard the call on dispatch—even though he wasn't on-site. He took it upon himself to go to the arena. When he arrived, he had to kick eight adults out of the ambulance before enlisting his one-year EMT student, Ethan, to help him intubate Shane. Chris knew exactly what was happening, and together, they took immediate action. We were losing him.

At the time, I didn't know all this, but I knew something needed to happen. The crew that had taken their sweet time had closed the doors to the ambulance in my face, telling me they were going to take him to Mineral Wells, where he surely and no doubt would have died. I got on the phone with longtime friend Shelly Mowery, who still has the recording of me asking her to call me back. She did, and I asked, "Hey, where is the number one trauma hospital in the Metroplex?"

She said, "JPS, John Peter Smith Hospital in Fort Worth."

I said, "Well, that's where we need to go." But all the while, I didn't know what Chris was doing inside. Only later did we find out that, at the same time, Chris was calling for dispatch and a life flight. And out of all that noise and commotion, he looked up and saw a helicopter flying overhead. He asked dispatch, "Who's that?"

"It's Eastland." Normally, they don't fuel up there, but they said, "They're here to fuel up and will be there in 10 minutes."

I believe it only took five minutes. Chris was dating a sweet little girl from JPS, and he was on the radio with her the whole time. We got JPS. The helicopter was on its way. We knew where we were headed.

Chris recalls:

"On the day of Shane's accident, it was an abnormal day of being busy. The day we heard the call out for Shane's accident, we were at a wreck near the golf course that had multiple crews swapped around. Staffing was short, so I cleared the accident and went to the rodeo grounds for the EMS call.

LOOK UP

Once to the grounds, I was directed to the ambulance on sight. As soon as I stepped into the ambulance, I knew it was a severe brain injury and quickly noted to the crew in the ambulance. Shane had decorticate posturing. The doors of the ambulance were open with spectators and unknown volunteer fire department personnel in the ambulance. Inside was pure chaos, and I quickly made all personnel other than the lead medic get out of the ambulance, and I closed the doors.

Mineral Wells Ambulance arrived on scene, and I quickly gave Ethan Weathers a run-down of what we had going on, and we made the decision to fly Shane to the closest trauma facility that was in Fort Worth. We controlled C-spine and moved Shane quickly to Mineral Wells ambulance. The decision was made by Weathers and me that Shane needed to be RSI'd (Rapid Sequence Intubated). I left Weathers to lead the EMS portion of the call in the Mineral Wells Ambulance, and I called for an air evac. I would periodically check in with the EMS crew and see if anything was needed. I was then told that no air evac unit was available for flight. I then contemplated what my next route was and was about to ask for a PHI or Care Flite helicopter when I looked up and noticed a helicopter that closely resembled an air evac helicopter with the red, white, and blue paint design.

I quickly got a hold of dispatch and asked what helicopter was dispatched, and they notified me that it was an Eastland or Abilene helicopter that was stopping at the Mineral Wells base for fuel. I asked if they would take the flight due to it being a severe brainstem injury and informed them that the patient was intubated. Air evac accepted the flight, with a turnaround of 10 minutes for refueling. I then went to the landing zone I chose, next to the softball field at the high school. The medic crew quickly came, and I was contacted on the radio by the pilot of the air evac that it was a two-minute ETA. The helicopter landed shortly after. The transition to move Shane to the helicopter happened quickly, and he was then sent off to JPS hospital.

On a day of pure chaos, with Mineral Wells Fire having multiple incidents and crews swapping roles multiple times, much good prevailed. Weathers was a new paramedic and did amazing and provided the best service any person could have. I don't think the outcome would have been the same without such an amazing crew and God working on our side."

We got in Liz's car, and she drove us to JPS. We came in so close to the helicopter that we had to wait for Shane to come down off the roof. He was so bad it took a while to get him stable enough to get him from the helicopter to full assessment care. We waited, looking up for him to get off of that roof for so long. I can honestly say that whenever I hear a helicopter, I stop and pray for whoever it is because I know it's bad.

Before Shane left the arena, there had been cowboys just standing there —one world champion in particular, Tuf Cooper, just prayed by the ambulance as the whole arena prayed. I have so many people who later contacted us to tell us what they felt that day.

But that evening, as we were dealing with it, Liz stayed with us. There were other people there, and though the rule was that only two people at a time could go back to see a patient, they allowed 12 of us to go back and pray over Shane. The purpose being from their mindset that Shane was about to die, and they were bending the two-person rule for a "hail mary" by allowing the 12 of us to pray.

But he was still posturing. That wasn't a good thing. After the prayer, Jim and I were called in to speak with the doctor. He had his computer out to show us the evidence. He informed us the injury was a diffuse axonal brain injury and that it was closing the butterfly in his brain because he had suffered what would be described as a complete brain shear, and it was bleeding. It was like a million fragile glass pipettes were shattered into a million pieces. He told us that if his brain didn't stop bleeding, he wouldn't be able to equalize the pressure, and Shane would die. Shane only had 10 percent pressurization left before that would happen. I don't know how, but I am so grateful for the motivation of love that let the Holy Spirit inspire me and give me confidence that the Lord would help me fight for my son's life—He told me to not give up.

> *"You shall not be terrified of them; for the Lord your God,*
> *the great and awesome God is among you."*
> **—Deuteronomy 7:21 NKJV**

As a fighting mom, I was propelled into immediate action, even in the midst of shock. My next move was confronting Dr. Gandhi, the leading brain specialist at JPS, by poking him in the chest and saying, "Yeah, but with brain injury, you don't know," as he laid out all the grim predictions. He spoke of the horrific outcomes—the likelihood that Shane would never walk or talk again, and how death was likely imminent, either in a few hours or days. He listed the countless complications that were "bound to happen" from this accident: bedsores, a cascade of medical issues, and a litany of disclaimers that sounded more like curses to me.

But the Bible tells us that life and death are in the power of the tongue. In that moment, I had a choice: to stand on God's promises or to believe the experts of this world. There wasn't an ounce of me ready to give up, because if Shane was meant to leave us, he would have died right there in the arena or on the way to the hospital. I believed the very fact that we made it to JPS was a miracle in itself, proof that God was prepared to do more.

As a mom, I dismissed the doctor's human authority because they don't truly understand what God can do. The unfolding events already pointed to something greater, and I chose to place my faith in Him rather than in the dire predictions of man.

> *"The name of the Lord is a strong tower;*
> *The righteous run to it and are safe."*
> **—Proverbs 18:10 NKJV**

I thank our mighty God that we're able to tell this story. Shane's living proof that you don't have to give up. You don't have to take the facts as they are until God tells you in your spirit, in your connection with him, when it's time to take the next step, no matter what that may be. We know that sometimes our healing is in heaven. There's nothing to be afraid of when you die when you believe in Jesus Christ. But, if we're supposed to stay here, to glorify God and be the miracles on this earthly time, then so be it. Let God use us equipped with His Word because it is the same today, yesterday, and forever. It's living proof of the miracles He performed. He's capable if we only believe. I see God as being handcuffed to the side of our lives sometimes, because all we want to do is speak cursing of what is happening in the natural that the enemy is using on this earth to come against us. We must realize that the sole effort of satan is to make us question and doubt God. We are called to say, "YES, Lord," not "Yes, satan." Thank you, Lord, for your Word, which reminds us of your promises. Our words carry power, for just as He spoke the universe into existence, we, too, speak blessings and healing—or the opposite.

Scripture calls us to bridle our tongues, and may God be glorified through our words. There is an enemy that sought to take Shane out, but God had something different to say about it. In our weakness, He will use us for His glory.

> *"Concerning this thing I pleaded with the Lord three times that it might depart from me. And He said to me, 'My grace is sufficient for you, for My strength is made perfect in weakness.' Therefore I take pleasure in infirmities, in reproaches, in needs, in persecutions, in distresses, for Christ's sake. For when I am weak, then I am strong."*
> —II Corinthians: 12:8-10 NKJV

Forcing things in life helps the negative. We can make our plans, but God designs our steps. Bad choices can bring bad consequences because you are no doubt out of God's will. It is not God's will to harm. That's a fact. Putting yourself in harm's way is not a choice God wants for us. Wanting something beyond the opportunities He has placed before us often means trying to control things that are beyond our power. When plans are made, but a "loose steer" or a misstep occurs in an effort to force something to happen, the result can lead to consequences that may even be fatal. The first days, his eyes remained shut—sometimes only slightly open—but he was still posturing, which means he was still showing signs of leaving us.

Shane has always wanted to be a light of Christ. I just don't think he knew to what degree. The spiritual fight that comes with staying tough when it gets tough sent me into overdrive. I watched the battle transpire; they sent clergy my way. Seeing as I was born and raised by a family of faith and my dad's father, my grandfather, a Baptist preacher, I took the responsibility of learning what that Word said for myself. I learned to be proud of where I came from, because I had the truth of what the maker of the universe had said.

Having learned that, I felt well-equipped when the clergy came to prepare Shane for death. If they were there to help me accept such a thing, I was ready to fight back with the Word. However, if they were there to stand in agreement with me, they were welcome to stay and speak blessings and Scripture over my son and be in agreement. Only under those conditions were they allowed and welcomed to remain.

The first lady quickly left, almost retreating on her heels. I suppose I scared her, but that's because I know my Jesus, and I know what He can do. As a stage three ovarian survivor who was already supposed to be gone, my son could survive, as well. I told the second guy from the clergy they sent around the same thing.

And guess what? He finally decided to get in agreement with what he was preaching—the Word. You can't come around representing the Bible and not stand in agreement with it, especially with a mother clinging to life, because my boy was not dead. He was in there, and they had to decide what to do with him. So, he stood in agreement with me.

Our pastor, Werth Mayes, and Associate Pastor Gene had arrived at the hospital, and we prayed together. I don't recall the words that were spoken but I do know exactly what we were believing. We stood firm in agreement. Your yes must be your yes, and your no must be your no. You can't waver when it comes to digging in during hard times. You can't say, "Well, I don't know." There's no belief or commitment in that. As cowboys and believers, we know the power of standing firm. Jim was most deeply moved when Werth prayed with us for a miracle—and we received one, one step at a time.

We were proving it. The bleeding stopped, and from that moment on, the butterfly in his brain did not change for the worse. It was beautiful to start watching it because after I asked the doctor to leave, I made the staff that was left in the room pray with us.

I remember the nurses coming in, some of them not believing the best. It stayed that way for quite some time because our battle was just starting, just to get through the first of many experiences. *Well, he didn't die today.* His buddy Kodie Jang from Australia had shown up before most everyone else. He dropped what he was doing in Snyder, Texas, drove there in the night, and stood next to Shane. This is Shane's favorite part of the story that he doesn't remember but we later told him—proof of survival, if you will. It comes in "naughty boy-talk" form. The nurse asked Kodie why he knew Shane was going to be okay. Kodie's response was, "Watch this." And he turned to Shane and went, "Hey, MF-er." Shane's reaction in the moment let everyone know that he heard him, as his monitors were immediately affected. They then politely asked Kodie to leave the room because they were trying to keep the brain pressure down at that time.

It makes Shane laugh because that's how some boys talk to one another. They say obscenities and punch each other in the arm, and this is how you communicate. The monitors were our only gauge of progression during his first days, as he wasn't moving or talking, partly due to the heavy sedation intended to prevent the pressure from increasing. Kodie is the toughest boy I know, even though Australians are known to be tough, and having that fun fact for Shane to laugh and giggle about and for them to remember is a lot better than what was about to happen. Even Kodie was standing in agreement.

You never know how strong you are until being strong is the only choice you have. Shane's going to be okay. We have to believe it because everybody was struggling. He began to have obstacles right away; there were trach placement troubles. The brain probe was off the charts, scaring everyone to pieces, as well. He had a botched feeding tube at the time. It wasn't working. They needed to do a second surgery. The highs and lows of those first few days were unbelievable because they were terrorizing every day.

I had to stand on hope, even when everybody else was fading. I remember the surrounding people, the nurses and staff, looking at me like I was in denial. *How pitiful. She needs to get ready for what could happen.* However, not all the nurses were like that. We had a fun bunch who were tired of seeing Shane with half his head shaved and a probe sticking out. Shane had these long, beautiful locks he had grown out, and one night, these sweet nurses decided to have a little spa session.

Since we never left Shane's side—either Jim or I was always with him—Jim got to hear the excitement of the nurses helping Shane look better. Jim handled the nights better since he could sleep in a recliner, while I took the daytime shift, ensuring someone was always there.

I asked Jim, "Did you get any rest?"

He replied, "Not really. We had a sorority party."

Confused, I said, "Excuse me?"

He explained, "Yeah, the girls decided they needed to clean him up. They cut his hair and gave him a little Fu Manchu shave."

Shane looked so handsome, so beautiful. It was fitting for the sharp-dressed man that he is. We got such a good laugh out of those nurses. But more than that, they were the ones who believed with us. They prayed with us, stayed in agreement with us, and never gave up hope—even when the brain probe started to malfunction.

It was just another terrorizing way to keep us all in disbelief. But I refused, I refused. At some point, you have to decide who you are going to believe in. And I know that there were prayers from Florida, California, Canada, Mexico, Australia, and beyond, throughout the PRCA world. We could feel it. We could feel the covering amongst all the darkness that was around us. JPS hospital was in a rough part of town. And the pandering was all around us. Some days I would help. Other days, I'd tell them what my son was going through. And they would end up praying with me and praying for him. For us. I let the Holy Spirit guide me. One day, I chased a homeless man down and gave him the food I was planning to keep that night when I got home from the hospital. I don't know why. I don't know why. But when you are showing God, if you want me to do that, if that's what you're saying, I'll do it.

When you want to follow that voice that says, *I don't know why I'm doing this. I don't know why I'm doing this, but it's for the greater good.* It's okay to follow it. Who cares if they think you're crazy? Because if God gives you miracles, it'll make their head spin. Let them think you're crazy because they'll see. They'll see that it's by the grace of God, and has nothing to do with your sanity and all about your obedience. While we were in the hospital, tortured day in and day out, there were some days that I had my head up, and I was speaking Jesus' faithfulness; other days, I had my head down, just repeating His name every day. I was staying super obedient to the promptings.

In that way, I felt that hedge of protection that wasn't allowing the total darkness to just engulf us. At one point, I had to get Jim in agreement with me. All in. I remember standing in the parking garage, and I told him he either had to believe with me, or I wasn't going to let him stand around and be around Shane like that—doubting until the evidence proved otherwise. I didn't let anybody outside of the medical staff in Shane's room who wasn't of radical, beautiful faith and trust. Allowing Jim to do the opposite was defeating the purpose.

Those who said, "Oh, I hope he gets better," with any hint of pity—I wouldn't tolerate it. Such words invited a spirit of giving up, and we couldn't afford that. We were in the trenches. When you're at the bottom of the hill, giving up isn't an option. There's too much mountain left to climb. You only let go of the climb when you've reached the top and can slide down the other side, laughing all the way.

That's when you can surrender it all—let go and let God. Let Him allow you to fully embrace the moment, to recognize that you *survived* and *made it*.

Jim and I had to have that come-to-Jesus meeting so that he could carry the weight of his own faith. He had to do it himself—not just *hope* but truly believe. He had to take responsibility for his own trust in God and the Scriptures, just as he did in life.

Before Jim and I had our little talk in the garage, I had all the noise around from those with pity. Out of nowhere, one day, the father of Micah Fox, a college friend of Shiloh's and Shane's, who I'd never met, showed up in the hallway. In his hand was a book of Jodie Osteen's healing book of prayers. Right there in that hallway, while those nurses with their cynicism were looking on, we stopped and prayed in front of everybody. He spoke a blessing over Shane that he would walk out of JPS hospital.

I needed just one other human being to quit messing around and get busy, to stay constant and unwavering and unafraid to go ahead and believe in the best when we had everything to lose. Why would you not want to believe in the best thing that could happen? If the worst happens? Big deal. Heaven for them, and the promises for us. But what if we're right? He lives and heals and glorifies!

That's when Jim and I had to have our little talk—because, for the first time, I had someone outside of our immediate world who actually agreed with me. I had been holding on to a different kind of denial—the idea that somehow Shane couldn't allow himself to *not* hope for a complete comeback.

No matter how deep in the trenches we were, no matter what the factual evidence showed, and no matter how insurmountable the mountain seemed, we **unapologetically** asked God to move it. I think I denied hopelessness completely. I just *refused* to accept it. Because Shane was still alive, and that alone was enough to believe in what God could do.

It was time to pause, take a breath, and say God's name: *Yahweh. Yahweh, Yahweh, Yahweh.* Every breath we take says His name. As long as your heart is beating and you're still breathing, life remains. Perhaps we're helping him because there was no evidence that we should stop. Use the stages of grief in a way that best supports life—whether it's moving forward without them while holding onto faith, or using those stages to create a better future. Even at worst, it's only waiting to see them in heaven, if God says it's time. It's all hope-filled because there is no downside to heaven and eternity.

We continued to prop each other up. Gradually, God kept doing so much, and Jim began reading the Bible to Shane at night; it was a wonderful thing to watch him not live in fear. It says to fear not in the Bible 365 times, one for every day of the year we get. 365 days or 365 times in the Bible, it says, "thou shall not fear" in one way or another.

It is so important to not fear because there's no room for it when you're fighting for the life of your child; there's nothing that can make you fearful. You have to be willing to pour hope into yourself. I refused to give up purposeful hope, and Jim followed suit. It was glorious in a way that only God could provide. The only bargaining stage of grief that I had was the singular moment in the hotel, screaming in the mirror for God's glory to prove all the disbelief wrong. That's what I was praying for. The wailings to the Lord of, *You know what You can do.* Screaming, "I want this horrible situation to show your glory so much that all people who are in doubt or disbelief are humbled!" That's what I was bargaining for because He didn't have to wait for me to be on board with what He could do! It was my choice to simply believe first and fight for the rest with God's help, responsible for the recount of the truth of God. He would need to continue revealing His power and bringing healing to fruition so that the rest of the "doubting Thomases" could be proven wrong in their assumptions. I vowed to remain faithful to the promptings of my heart through the lens of what the Bible had taught me. I did stuff that I thought at the time seemed crazy, but I was so moved to listen and hear from the ultimate helper, The Holy Spirit, that I was completely usable by God. I felt others' disbelief. It was palatable to me. Some were just there to prepare to bury Shane anyway.

"But Jesus turned around, and when He saw her He said, "Be of good cheer, daughter; your faith has made you [your son] well." And the woman was made well from that hour."
—Matthew 9:22 NKJV

But I vowed to remain faithful and unwavering in my trust in God that He would grant Shane life, and we didn't stop fighting for every bit of that, asking and praying and trusting and believing and standing on God's promises and in His Word. Believing God would continue to bring divine intervention, not unlike Chris, not unlike when the insurance was telling me I wouldn't be qualified to get him where I was trying to get him, which was Baylor Rehab in Dallas. Shane wasn't well enough. And the insurance didn't qualify. I worked, and I worked, and I kept calling, and kept calling, and I finally got a miraculous girl on the phone—Miss Kendra, I'll never forget. And she says, "You're not going to believe this, but that just changed and is now in the realm of usage."

I don't care what you believe, but I'll claim it as another little miracle —God saying, *"Okay, stay hooked."* We started preparing Shane for the next step so he could get well. See, I didn't just think he was going to survive. I didn't think we'd simply be taking care of him. We were getting him all the way back because if you don't ask God for the most in the world, then what are you doing? You're limiting Him. God wants to give us far more than we could ever think, imagine, or feel. Wrap your mind around that. So, when you want to dream big and aim high, you'd better include God. If you're going to leave Him out, then don't even bother trying.

"God is our refuge and strength, a very present help in trouble. Therefore we will not fear, Even though the earth be removed, And though the mountains be carried into the midst of the sea."
—Psalms 46:1-2 NKJV

My bargaining was a plea for God to prove them all wrong—all the experts. Chris was the first of many wonders, just like the insurance. It can only be explained by the grace of God. No human could have orchestrated what was happening or made possible what seemed impossible.

While we were at the hospital, the darkness was palpable. So many people were hurting, and as the saying goes, hurting people hurt people. When we step back, resist taking things personally, and ask, "Why are you hurting so much?" we might soften their hearts enough for them to address their pain rather than project it onto others.

There was a young man at the check-in desk. I said, "Excuse me, boy," because he was younger than me, and I often refer to younger men as cowboys. This didn't sit well with him. He took offense, and a girl at the desk stepped in to diffuse the situation. Later, I went around the corner and confided in her about what I'd wanted to say, though we both agreed it was better that I hadn't. In the moment, I didn't give it much thought—I simply returned to Shane and went about my day.

In the days that followed, however, that man made his feelings clear. Everywhere I sat in the waiting room, he would follow me and flip me off repeatedly with his chosen finger.

Whoever I was sitting with, I would just share stories of God's grace and what Jesus was doing in our lives with Shane's situation. So, while that man sat flipping me off and following me around, he had to listen to me talk about how Jesus was working miracles for my son. He followed me until the day we were able to take Shane home from JPS. Security had to escort me to the car for safety since Jim rode in the ambulance with Shane.

By that point, Shane had already undergone his second surgery on his trach and another on his feeding tube. We had qualified to move him to an interim facility in Dallas until he was well enough to transition to Baylor. But through all of this, nothing or no one brought about fear. I simply knew the enemy was working hard to oppose us, and that I didn't have time to worry about any of it. My son needed our focus and care, and I refused to give that man much attention.

Looking back, I realize it was a wonderful way for God to help me handle the situation. I was humbled that I didn't let my fleshly instincts take over and give a lecture the likes of that every young adult who might need to know Jesus better should hear. Instead, God kept my focus on sharing His incredible work—how He was healing our son and bringing about the next miracles as we continued to speak blessings over our lives.

LOOK UP

> *"Cast your burden on the Lord, And He will sustain you;*
> *He shall never permit the righteous to be moved."*
> **—Psalms 55:22 NKJV**

Although things were still bad, we continued to speak blessings. And when Shane locked eyes with my niece, Robin Montague, I knew he was in there. This was the day of long-awaited validation.

When he looked at Robin that day, the way his eyes saw her, I knew he was all there, regardless of how he could communicate it, even if they said his brain was ripped in half or whatever the evidence showed. I knew we had our Shane. Jim was given that glimmer of hope in the ambulance when they left JPS and headed to Dallas. The guy in the ambulance told Jim that Shane was tracking him with his eyes—Shane couldn't move yet, but he was looking up and tracking his daddy with his eyes.

This journey has nothing to do with hopelessness. When you deny hopelessness, you reject what the enemy intends to do to you. As it says in John 10:10, "The thief comes only to steal, kill, and destroy."

> *"The thief does not come except to steal, and to kill, and to destroy.*
> *I have come that they may have life, and that they*
> *may have it more abundantly."*
> **—John 10:10**

Jesus came so that we may have life and have it in abundance and to the full. But things were about to get even tougher.

CHAPTER 4
STAY HOOKED

"Be kindly affectionate to one another with brotherly love, in honor giving preference to one another; not lagging in diligence, fervent in spirit, serving the Lord; rejoicing in hope, patient in tribulation, continuing steadfastly in prayer; distributing to the needs of the saints, given to hospitality."
—Romans 12:10-13 NKJV

"Good enough" was not good enough. Complete restoration, in the name of Jesus, was the goal. Not just anyone was allowed to pray over Shane or even see him, because I was in a protective, spiritual mode—we were just getting started.

After the officers had gotten me safely to my car and following behind Jim and Shane in the ambulance, we made the drive from Fort Worth to Dallas to a hospital that worked in conjunction with Baylor. It had its own specialized floor called Select. As we walked through the doors, we were greeted by the wonderful Kathee Horn. She told us that she had been praying for Shane even before we met her. She explained her connection to the PBR (Professional Bull Riders) and the rodeo world and how she had seen his picture.

In that moment, we immediately knew that God was, once again, sending us the comfort and confirmation we needed. We were on the right path.

TRINA POWERS-HADLEY

KATHEE HORN'S LETTER

My name is Kathee Horn, and this is how I met the one and only Shane Hadley and how I became a part of his miracle story.

My background as a nurse is in trauma/critical care. I was a flight nurse and wound care educator and director. I was raised and involved within the horse and rodeo industry from a young age. And in my adult age, I enjoy giving back to the rodeo industry that has given me so much by contributing my time and supplies to rodeo sports medicine. As I am sure you have come to find, the rodeo industry is a large but close-knit family. You almost always know everyone, or if you don't know them, then they usually know of you, or you know someone who knows them. It is truly a blessing to be a part of something so vast yet small in its own little way.

On May 12th, 2018, I was out celebrating my youngest daughter's 21st birthday when I received a text message saying, "Pray for one of our own. Pray for Shane, who was injured at the Mineral Wells Rodeo tonight." I immediately shared the message with everyone I knew and began praying for healing and for his family. I followed his story and kept up with continued prayers for their strength and healing.

Fast forward to early June 2018, I was working as a director at a hospital in Dallas, Texas. Case management had called me and asked if I could stay late and do an admission of a patient who would be coming in late that evening. I said of course I could, even though admissions weren't a part of my day-to-day responsibilities. I had no name of the patient or information at that time. Later that evening, I was in my office, and the unit secretary called me and told me that the patient had arrived via stretcher and was in the room with all the paperwork that needed to be completed.

Upon entering the room, I saw Jim, Shane's father, standing on the other side of the bed. Shane lay emaciated with his head shaven. He was so thin; his muscles had started to shrink from him not using them. Prior to the accident, Shane was in very good shape, which is probably what helped him sustain so long and so well in his condition. Shane had been intubated and was on a ventilator at the previous hospital, and he had a tracheostomy for breathing. I looked at Jim and said, "Mineral Wells, May 12th?" This started our conversation, and we conversed until Jim's wife and Shane's mother, Trina, arrived from the emergency room, where Shane had arrived via ambulance from the prior hospital.

When I met Trina, it was an immediate connection. Here this family was that I had been praying endlessly for, a divine intervention. We conversed as I did Shane's intake paperwork, and we quickly realized we knew so many of the same people, even though prior to living in Texas, I had lived in South Dakota for several years. Shane had been born in South Dakota; the connections were never-ending. Because of my immediate bond with the Hadleys, I felt it was a calling for me to be an advocate for Shane, which wasn't unusual in my line of work, but this felt different.

Upon my assessment, I found an abdominal incision wound that was from a failed feeding tube placement, which occasionally happens. We had plans for another surgery at our facility to place a feeding tube. Shane had not eaten since his accident due to the traumatic brain injury, but being intubated and on the ventilator, this was totally normal with someone in Shane's condition, and he had been receiving nutrients via IV.

I completed my assessment, got Shane tucked in for the night, and made sure Jim and Trina were comfortable and understood the next steps. I advised them that I would be back in the morning and to get some well-needed rest. On my long commute home that night and while feeding my horse, I could not stop thinking of how this must be God's work for our paths to cross like this.

When I arrived the next morning at the hospital, I went to check on Shane, Trina, and Jim. Upon my morning assessment of his abdominal wound, I found signs of infection. Being this was Friday, I knew it could not wait until the weekend. I called one of our surgeons to come up and look at Shane. The surgeon arrived, and Shane was prepped for surgery immediately and started on antibiotics. If Shane's surgery would have been prolonged, he could have become septic, which can turn bad quickly and lead to other complications, including death. When Shane arrived back from the operating room, I examined the site and reviewed the wound care orders. There is no wound care provided on the weekends, so I taught Trina how to do Shane's dressing changes and left her the needed supplies. I informed the staff to allow Trina to call me during the weekend with any questions or concerns.

TRINA POWERS-HADLEY

We spent lots of time that weekend on calls managing Shane's wound and drainage from the wound. The surgeon even came and checked on Shane over the weekend, which is not a normal routine. Shane's incision healed beautifully with minimal scarring. A feeding tube was placed the following week without any complications.

I was so impressed by Shane's parents, Jim and Trina, for never leaving his side, despite his mother battling cancer and his father having Parkinson's. He was literally never without at least one of them, and I highly suggest this to all my patients: always have a family member or an advocate with you in the hospital. A whole rodeo family came together, a whole support system of family and friends to pray and care for Shane. Everyone rallied around Shane and brought hope and positive attitudes to the bedside daily.

Shane and his family faced many challenges daily; the devil was hard at work for sure. We faced them together. Shane needed a larger room in a more secluded, quieter area of the floor, so he had less stimulation for his healing brain. When the perfect room opened, I requested to have him moved. I was able to advocate this with lots of pushback from staff. We prevailed, and he was able to heal in a quieter space.

Trina had asked if we could put the essential oil juices in Shane's feeding tube to promote healing. I am a true believer in the essential oils treatments and have witnessed amazing outcomes using them. While other staff members were ignoring Trina's request, I took the product to my case management meeting and met with the dietician to discuss using it in the feeding tube for Shane. After review and discussion with Shane's physician it was approved, and an order was written that he be given the essential oils juice via feeding tube twice daily. Due to this, I witnessed an improvement in Shane after this was started.

I had placed a three-point turning system on Shane so he would not develop pressure injuries, and Trina and I faithfully turned him every two hours. Trina would joke that we were turning him like a rotisserie chicken. Shane could not communicate at this time, and by the looks he would give me I could tell he was not happy; I would tell him, "I know you don't like me now, but you will someday." When Shane started improving, he threw a pillow at me, and I knew then he was improving.

LOOK UP

With Shane's Traumatic Brain Injury (TBI), he had decorticate posturing, where the wrists curl and hands ball to the chest. Shane's left hand remained like this for some time. I was on my way home one evening from work and stopped at the Christian bookstore and bought a palm cross, which is a wooden cross that fits in the palm of your hand for Shane to hold.

Every time I entered Shane's room, you would feel the presence of peace and a bigger power. I could feel the prayers working; it is something you can't explain, but you have to experience. I have witnessed many amazing, humbling events in my career and life, but people take so much for granted daily. To witness a family keep hope, faith and strength through a trial like this was truly amazing; they were all so resilient.

There were times I would approach the room and could hear them praying over Shane; I would wait outside and pray, too, and there were times I would pray with them around Shane. I always felt the sense of God's presence in that room. Being with Shane daily, I was able to witness the small improvements he was making, and it was so rewarding. I remember opening the door one morning early and seeing Jim and Trina sleeping on a small chair in the room together. Usually, one would go to the apartment that they had rented near the hospital and sleep while the other stayed. I said, "What are you two doing? That can't be very comfortable," and Trina said, "Today is our wedding anniversary, so we wanted to be together." I loved that.

We became family through that journey, and Shane is my hero. Most would have given up, but not the "Rockstar Cowboy."

I remember the day Shane was being discharged from my hospital to go through the underground tunnel to the rehabilitation hospital. Trina said they were leaving all the struggles and darkness there and moving forward to more positive improvements, and we all prayed.

We are now family, and I have continued this healing journey with the Hadleys. They are a blessing. I feel I was placed exactly where I was supposed to be at just the right time, and I am so glad that God chose me to travel this journey with them. We are where we are supposed to always be, placed on the path he has chosen for us—even if we do not understand the journey or the path, it is in his great timing.

We knew he was hurt badly, and that the only thing we could do was not limit what God could do. Our every step had to start with belief. If you don't first believe, then you can't trust. If you don't trust, there's nothing to stand on. And if you can't stand on the promises written in his holy word and in the Bible, then what will you cling to? When Jim would read those Bible Scriptures, it helped him stand in agreement and remember the moments, like when Shane looked at Robin, when we knew he was there and to keep battling for him. But he was sick, and he was hurt badly. What we found out was that his misplaced feeding tube was misplaced again. And so instead of just moving into Select and starting to prepare to get better, we weren't done yet. I just kept denying that he couldn't heal.

We were in the scariest parts. I was determined to make sure that we did the next right thing.

When we arrived at Select, we knew Shane was not doing well. We had been using essential oils on him since the beginning—Frankincense being the number one oil for brain injuries. We applied it to his big toes to help oxygenate his brain, as that's the reflexology point for the brain.

The woman, Judy, who guided us, was also very knowledgeable about essential oils and their benefits. She sensed something was wrong in Shane's abdomen and shared her concerns with Robin.

Looking back, I remember the second surgery for Shane's feeding tube at JPS. The young surgeon seemed so nervous, her clenched fists opening and closing as she explained the procedure. In that moment, I had a sense that her nerves might lead to a mistake. Reflecting on it now, I feel certain that's exactly what happened.

On Jim and my 30th wedding anniversary, we were trying to get Shane settled when he started coughing. Each time he coughed, the abscess from the misplaced feeding tube began gushing fluid through the stitches in his abdomen, squirting out everywhere.

Rather than leaving him to the overworked and understaffed medical team, we stayed by his side. We never left him, sharing a tiny wooden bench-bed, head to toe, even though we rarely laid down. That night, we got up nine times to change the bandages on his abdomen, ensuring he wouldn't suffer a skin breakdown.

He was scheduled for surgery the next day, but this moment was probably the most sobering for me. It was when everything felt incredibly serious—real serious.

Even though I knew that if Shane couldn't overcome this hurdle, we would have to prepare ourselves for everything—the curses and doubts people had been speaking over us. How did I respond to that? I didn't settle. I let it bother me for a moment, cried briefly, and then moved forward. Seeing Shane curled up in the fetal position reminded me of my dad before he passed away from cancer—the resemblance was striking.

The next thing I remember is my great nephew, Sam Powers, arriving with money to rent an apartment, thanks to my brother, Jimmy, and other great friends. We were going to stay in the city. Blessings beyond blessings were happening at home and in the background. People were giving so much—they cared for our animals, managed our home, and found accommodations for us, including a month-to-month rental apartment.

For Shane's protection and advocacy, Jim and I took shifts, trading day and night so that someone was always with him. My brother sent money to cover the rent, and my nephew dropped it off, he was so nervous he couldn't stay long.

I remember walking back in and seeing Shane. He looked so much like my dad in his final stages. Shane had become emaciated, 62 pounds lighter, hadn't eaten in 21 days, and was fighting for his life—not just to survive surgery but also to recover from the brain injury. It was incredibly sobering.

I remember praying, asking God to be with the surgeon, guiding Dr. Warren's hands.

> *"Do not remember the former things, nor consider the things of old.*
> *Behold, I will do a new thing, Now it shall spring forth;*
> *Shall you not know it? I will even make a road*
> *in the wilderness and rivers in the desert."*
> **—Isaiah 43: 18-19 NKJV**

All glory to God that Shane survived the much-needed surgery. We were grateful to have Kathee because, without her, we'd have had no abdication in the most heinous facility we endured. I don't mind calling them out—Select was horrible to us. The staff constantly fought among themselves, trying to one-up each other, with more concern for their own interests than for their patients, even arguing over whether we could have a certain room. The patients are comatose; they're left there alone.

The mentality of much of the staff seemed to be to go around, check the bare minimum boxes, and carry out their monotonous routines, undisturbed by loved ones watching over their patients. There was an unspoken arrogance—a sense that they were in no hurry.

By this time, we were closely monitoring Shane ourselves. We could see every time he was in pain after surgery because his vitals would spike on the monitors. The staff questioned us, asking how we knew that—but how could we not? It had been eight hours!

When Kathee wasn't there, it was nearly impossible to have any abdication. I felt like Sally Field in that movie where her daughter is dying of cancer, desperately wanting to ease her child's pain. I remember standing in the hallway, throwing my hat down the corridor just as she did, pleading with them to help my baby. "Please, just bring me his meds!"

Shane needed regular cleanup, but the staff's response system was far from effective. There was a screen that displayed when assistance was requested, which felt absurd given that most patients were alone and comatose. If they were alone, how could they call for help?

We would press the button for aid and cleanup, and the screen would track how long it took for someone to respond. Ninety-two minutes later, no one had arrived. Imagine if Shane had been left for that long—92 minutes without care. And they wonder why patients develop infections, skin breakdown, sores, and other complications they claim to battle. The truth is, without an advocate, these outcomes are inevitable.

Kathee, an expert in trauma care with decades of frontline experience, introduced us to a three-point turn system. Every two hours, we turned Shane like a rotisserie chicken to prevent sores and skin issues. Thanks to this diligent care, he only developed one tiny red mark on his backside the entire time he couldn't move.

From the very beginning, we did physical therapy with him—range-of-motion exercises—even though he couldn't participate. We anointed him with oils and went far beyond simply letting him lie there, subject to the grim statistics we saw down the hall.

Kathee was our saving grace. When the gushing wound happened in the middle of the night, we called her. Even though she wasn't on call and owed us nothing, she answered. She never left our side, and we are forever grateful for her unwavering support.

She's been the greatest guide. With her 40-plus years in the medical industry and being a specialist in wound care, she goes and speaks and teaches. We were blessed to have her helping us keep Shane from every one of those terrible statistics that they just flippantly lay out there like they should be accepted and not battled against. Kathee is irreplaceable.

The anger we felt during this accident fueled our determination to advocate for Shane. I remember the girl on call when it was finally time for Shane to receive some nourishment after the accident. It was day 21—I was begging her to come and turn his feeding tube on. She casually said she'd get around to it but needed to take her lunch break first. This man, who hadn't eaten in almost a month, had to wait because she couldn't take a moment out of her schedule to flip the switch so his feeding tube could run properly.

It wasn't as though I was disturbing anyone else—I was never reprimanded for screaming, hollering, begging, pleading, or even threatening—but we expected better from the staff. Because of situations like this, we stopped relying on them for anything beyond absolute necessities. Instead, we leaned on our "dream team": Ms. Evelyn, Ms. Kathee, and the others who remained committed to doing right by their patients. They refused to let the system jade or sour them to their oath of care, compassion, and the goal of recovery.

I honestly don't know how we would have managed without Kathee. She was a miracle worker, a constant reminder that we had to channel our grief productively—to move forward, stay strong, and continue thanking God for those He sent to help us.

The anger we felt wasn't because Shane was hurt—yes, we were sad and heartbroken, but the anger was directed toward those who refused to help us improve his condition. We were angry at the dismissive attitudes and the grim predictions spoken over him, like, "You'll need to buy a handicapped van because he'll be in a wheelchair." That anger burned just beneath the surface—not out loud, but deeply within. Because I didn't believe it. I refused to believe it.

And so, once again, the truth we allow into our lives is ultimately what we choose to believe. What we decide to accept as true must be measured against God's Word and what we're experiencing. I understand that we can't ignore reality—I'm not being irrational about that. What I'm asking is this: What will you stand on when you need it most?

Will it be the promises God has given us, or the hurt and pain the enemy tries to use to steal our hope, to kill, and to destroy? As it says in Scripture, the enemy is a fallen angel for a reason. His mission should fail, and it's already foretold—he's destined to be cast into the pit of hell, bound there for thousands of years. He is a defeated foe. That's what Scripture tells us—my Savior rules and reigns.

"You are My witnesses," says the Lord, and My servant whom I have chosen, that you may know and believe Me, and understand that I am He. Before Me there was no God formed, nor shall there be after Me. I, even I, am the Lord, And besides Me there is no savior."
—Isaiah 43: 10-11 NKJV

When the enemy is coming against you, admit that he's real and a joy stealer until the second coming of Christ. People don't understand and confuse themselves by falling for the lie that God made the harm. He may have allowed it—big difference. God never does any of the bad. God doesn't have any control over choice. It was a choice. Shane has had to deal with that hard, hard fact. It was his choice to be unsafe. He needed to pull up. He didn't. And he's paid the consequence for it.

You have to handle that with truth, not blame or even guilt. You have to decide: *what are you going to do with that truth?* What are you going to learn from it? Are you going to learn to keep pounding your head against that and say, "Oh, I can do it better if I try harder by myself next time?" Or do you listen to the promptings of the Holy Spirit, follow His guidance, and trust and believe that more can be done with God and for God being hurt than could be done by winning a prize?

The Bible says that prizes wither and fade. I don't mean to diminish the value of hard work—everyone loves excelling in sport. The drive to compete and win is neither dismissed nor disrespected in the least. But we must keep the right perspective: *What is the most important thing in life?*

You have to ask yourself whether it's to glorify God and become the most excellent version of what He created you to be, or to give in to the voices around you. What do you want to believe? What do you choose to believe?

We chose to believe that we wouldn't give in to the dire conditions or lose hope. In making that choice, we glorified our God in Heaven by saying, "I trust You, Lord—first, only, and always."

Like I said, not just anyone was allowed to pray over Shane. If they didn't come from a heart and voice of relentless release of faith and respectful reminders of what God's Word says of the promises He provided for our healing and strength, it wasn't allowed. The woes of questioning His will, if it be, was not in any request made to God from us. He loves and responds to those who can tell Him what He said to His chosen. Because of my simple faith to believe that Jesus came, died, and rose again for me to be a partaker in His chosen children is my honor, privilege and greatest choice for life in abundance, whether abased or abounding.

LOOK UP

"Not that I speak in regard to need, for I have learned in whatever state I am, to be content; I know how to be abased, and I know how to abound. Everywhere and in all things I have learned both to be full and to be hungry, both to abound and to suffer need. I can do all things through Christ who strengthens me."
—**Philippians 4: 11-13**

Often, this last little nugget of Scripture is taken out of context and used to suggest that we can simply do all things with God's strength. Yes, it says that, but if you read the context, you realize that God is with you in both the good and the bad. There's a balance—He helps you survive the bad and appreciate the good in real time. How wonderful it can be to use God's truth in that He is with you, instead of participating in years of self-abuse or whatever distraction or misconception that might be used to carry out the enemy's bidding in your life during times of difficulty.

My friend Colleen possesses unstoppable faith. I allowed her to pray over my son because she understands hardship. She and her husband, RC, have endured the greatest pain a parent can face.

When we met, I had just returned to Wyoming after burying my mom. She was 59 and passed away from a heart attack. Two weeks earlier, my sister-in-law had been in a car wreck, and two days after my mom's passing, she died from a blood clot. Despite never meeting me before, Colleen approached me to offer her condolences.

The next day, at a roping event, RC—one of the handiest and most humble cowboys I've ever known—was competing. RC wouldn't boast about it, but when he was younger, he was a stunt double in John Wayne's movie *The Cowboys*. He's broken and trained more horses than most people will ever see, and he taught his sons safety around horses, cattle, and ropes. They are true cowboys.

While Colleen and RC were at a team roping, their son Ryan was with his brother, Cole, and some other kids playing on the fence. A young, inexperienced man, his rope tied hard and fast to his saddlehorn, was showing off his self-professed "calf horse." The man had no neck rope or keeper on his horse's neck to keep the animal focused on what was at the end of the rope. With the rope around Ryan, the inexperienced man stepped off, and when he dismounted and asked the kids if they wanted to see his calf horse work, he lost control of the horse. Without the neck rope and keeper to keep the horse looking at Ryan, the horse turned and ran, dragging Ryan to his death in front of his parents, brother, and everyone at the team roping event.

The most painful thing was that the young boys knew how unsafe it was, but in the blink of an eye, some unknowing person produced tragedy. It was devastating for someone like RC, who had such deep knowledge being raised in western heritage, cowboy wisdom, and horse safety, who also had instilled that safety in his boys. It shows no matter how prepared we think we have made ourselves, we can still be vulnerable to the ignorance of others.

Unlike many couples who lose a child, Colleen and RC stayed together. They leaned on Christ and became a testament to what it means to persevere through the greatest loss imaginable—something beyond the natural order of life.

It was not how God intended. Yet, they turned to faith in the Lord. RC, by living it and quietly showing it, and Colleen, by praising Jesus out loud, always depending on Him. Faith like that never prosecuted the man and only gave grace and mercy to him for his ignorance and neglect of safety. The kind of warriors at the mercy of Christ that you want in your corner. RC is our number one roping and golf coach, and Colleen is my sister in Christ and warrior in Jesus. She came and prayed over Shane. Her faith is so unwavering and so strong that when she came in and prayed over Shane, it was the prayer that raised Jesus. She whispered in his ear, and he squeezed her hand, and he let her know he was there. It was another confirmation of hope since he hadn't been moving very much at all.

She said the following:

> *"But if the (same) Spirit of Him who raised Jesus from the dead dwells in you, He who raised Christ from the dead will also give life to your mortal bodies through His Spirit who dwells in you."*
> **—Romans 8: 11**

Shane looked up and had to know we weren't giving up because when we prayed over him, you could feel it. You could feel the presence of God.

COLLEEN DONALDSON'S LETTER

I had moved to Texas in the summer of 2018. Jim and Trina and I have been great friends since about 1994, having met at my All-Girls Rodeo at the Newcastle Spring Fling. I have to say that Trina is the most steadfast friend to have. She will go to bat for you on any level. I love her so much.

LOOK UP

I knew I needed to go see her and the family where Shane was hospitalized. I remembered Shane Hadley as a big, stout, good-looking young man who was so talented in rodeo, football, and just an all-around ranch family hand. They lived about 40 miles up the road from me.

When I walked in, I was met by the strongest mother anyone should have. I knew she was not going anywhere and she wasn't leaving without her son alive and well. I will not lie; I was taken aback by what I saw. Shane was lying there in what most would say in a dead stare. Curled up, 60 pounds lighter than normal. I love Jesus more than anything on this earth, and I heard the Holy Spirit say, "Tell him!" I don't care what anyone believes, but I knew the presence of almighty God was in that room.

I went to Shane and spoke these words in his ear. I was holding onto his limp hand.

If the same spirit that raised Jesus from the dead dwells in you, that same spirit that raised Jesus from the dead will quicken your mortal body and restore life unto you.

I knew he heard me because, at that very moment, he looked at me and, with his limp hand, began to squeeze mine. I knew he believed it.

We prayed over Shane and his family and commanded healing to come. One of the things I remembered was that Trina had literally run off the doctor who said he will never be okay. The next day, she called me and said they moved to rehab.

Healing began to move through his body. Myself, as well as thousands of the Hadley family's friends, waited nightly to read the daily journey of love that was all around this young man and his parents. I would wake up and read Trina's post for the day that she wrote usually at the midnight hour, after she was completely spent. Everyone I talked to said how they looked forward to the Daily Report of Shane because it was based on God's Word. Trusting God for knowledge, wisdom, understanding, peace, and believing all of God's promises of healing and restoration, forgiveness, and not accepting anything else. I have had people tell me they came or prayed hoping to bring comfort, but it was this mom and her journal that brought all of us comfort! What a blessing they have been to all.

CHAPTER 5
IN THE BOOGIE

*"A merry heart does good, like medicine,
but a broken spirit dries the bones."*
—Proverbs 17:22

Very early on, we realized the need to simplify communication about Shane's condition with our loved ones. Instead of answering endless texts and messages, I decided to commit to one Facebook post a day to keep everyone informed of Shane's progress. This served a dual purpose: sharing the Scripture we stood on and marking the day—a calendar of our journey, numbering each report with a focus only on the positives. We deliberately gave no unnecessary attention to the challenges happening behind the scenes.

These updates soon took on a life of their own—a lifeline. The posts became known as the infamous *Praise Reports*. My goal was simple: to praise every inch of progress God gave us. Alongside Scripture and even the smallest improvements to celebrate, we infused humor by naming the days creatively.

We had names like *Miracle Monday, Magnificent Monday, More Than Enough Monday*, and even *Macrocosmic Monday*. Tuesdays became *Terrific Tuesday, Transformational Tuesday, Ta-Da Tuesday,* and *Take A Step of Faith Tuesday*. On Wednesdays, we used *Workout Wednesday, Wow Them*

Wednesday, We All Wonder Why Wednesday, and *Wishes Come True Wednesday.* Thursdays included *Thrilled Thursday, Take Notice Thursday, Turn Up the Power Thursday,* and *Tenacious Thursday.*

Fridays inspired *Feisty Friday, Faith-Filled Friday, Fortunate Friday, Phenomenal Friday,* and *Full of Hope Friday.* Saturdays brought *Sassy Saturday, Stay Strong Saturday,* and *Still Working Saturday,* because even without therapists on weekends, Shane kept working—with just us. When creativity was running low, we embraced names like *Beyond Blessed Belmont Saturday.*

Sundays rounded things out with *Self-Motivated Sunday, Saved By Grace Sunday, Fiesta Siesta Sunday, Fun in the Son Sunday,* and *SonSational Sunday.* On days that called for a change, we mixed it up with names like *Feeling Fine on Day 79* or *Great Day 78.*

My favorite was after a major therapy breakthrough: *Throw Your Hands In The Air Like You Just Don't Care Tuesday*—and I didn't! By this point, the purpose of these posts was clear: glorify God and draw attention to the mighty works He was doing for us. They kept us pumped up, focused on what was going right, and constantly reminded us of the countless people praying with us. Truly, "Amazing things which Thou hast done!"

I don't know that I appreciated it in the moment as much as I see now how God's anointing was there. In the battle on the front lines, we were putting that armor on every day, and we all had to survive and know who we were in Christ. We were asking that from everyone—to realize the need for the helmet of salvation in the presence of our dire situation. A moment where one has to know who you are in Christ to protect your mind from what the enemy wants to drop in there, not unlike a spirit of doubt. We have no doubt when it comes to Christ.

We have the opportunity to read it for ourselves in the books compiled and written over generations to collectively give you—the Basic Instructions Before Leaving Earth, or the **BIBLE**.

Grab and take hold of the breastplate of righteousness referenced in Ephesians 6:10–20, knowing that we are saved by the blood of Jesus, that He loves us and desires no harm for us. With that assurance, the enemy couldn't make us blame God or retreat from the battle. After all, there's no armor for your backside—you're not meant to run. We didn't have time for that. Jesus is the one who saves us.

I believe the belt of truth stabilizes the core of everything, and standing in the shoes of peace, as described in Scripture, will either take you or keep you exactly where you need to be—in peace. We all have to decide for ourselves whether we will walk in His shoes of peace or throw them aside in opposition to God's peace.

The sword we are called to fight with is the Word of God. With it, we slice through every lie, attack, and deception the enemy tries to bring against us, standing firm and surviving on God's truth.

That's how we survived the worst of the facilities. We were surrounded by people who wouldn't take no for an answer and helped us do everything possible for Shane. Dr. Warden, who evaluated Shane regularly, was instrumental in determining when he was well enough to transition across the street to Baylor Rehab. She would come in and go, "That's good, Shane, but I want better." Not good enough, yet. We were getting there, but we had to go through the hardest trenches during the battle. I can't think how we would have done it without the help from those who wanted to be the hands and feet of God, who wanted to do the next right thing, who wanted to make sure that patients didn't go without their pain meds or that they didn't have to live in skin breakdown because they were well taken care of.

It is infuriating to hear what insurance will and won't cover. Who decides we can't start physical therapy yet? Not only did we have to fight for that, but we also had to plead with the staff to let us use oils and other methods we believed would help Shane get better. We have numerous PTs in our family, and we started range of motion physical therapy before Shane could even participate.

Frankincense (as I mentioned before, the number one essential oil for brain injury) has been proven to aid in healing. It was one of the three gifts brought to the Christ child at birth—frankincense, myrrh, and gold—and was considered more valuable than the gold. Why? Because Jesus would encounter countless people with illnesses and in need of healing, and He needed to stay well.

Genesis tells us that plants were put on the earth for our well-being. Frankincense, which means "God is with us," oxygenates the brain and promotes wellness of the mind. God wants our minds to be well so that our thoughts and eyes remain fixed on Him. Healing wasn't going to come through mediocrity. Miracles wouldn't happen with just enough effort. Choosing to look up from the depths, to step up in your faith—it's not for the faint of heart, nor can one be double-minded and back and forth. It requires complete faith and an unwavering, relentless pursuit of what God could do. And that's exactly what we fought for.

At Select, we learned that the hardest times brought us the greatest strength to keep going. That strength allowed us to begin truly embracing what was ahead—the real healing, the blessings, and the stories we were preparing to pray over this boy.

"For I consider that the sufferings of this present time are not worthy to be compared with the glory which shall be revealed in us. For we were saved in this hope, but hope that is seen is not hope; for why does one still hope for what he sees? But if we hope for what we do not see, we eagerly wait for it with perseverance. Likewise, the Spirit also helps in our weaknesses. For we do not know what we should pray for as we ought, but the Spirit Himself makes intercession for us with groanings which cannot be uttered. Now He who searches the hearts knows what the mind of the Spirit is, because He makes intercession for the saints according to the will of God. And we know that all things work together for good to those who love God, to those who are called according to His purpose."
—**Romans 8:18, 24-28**

We found ourselves doing everything we could to know that we had to keep our eyes on God and our thoughts on Him so that we were not distracted. We kept anointing Shane and praying over him with that frankincense. We just kept praying. You can see the light in His room, and when people would come in, they could feel the Holy Spirit. We began using a tilt table to help Shane. We would lay him flat, his body limp, and strap him securely from his head, shoulders, hips, thighs, and ankles. Then, we would stand him up using the inversion table, as he couldn't support himself at all.

He was so weak he couldn't even hold his head up. When we stood him up, his entire body had to be strapped in because he had no strength of his own. He was emaciated, having lost over 62 pounds—a mere skeleton of himself after being off his feet for so many days. He couldn't do much; even a simple thumbs-up was a struggle. But we prayed over him, clinging to every small move or sign of progress we could see.

I saw a difference. And so did everybody else after Shane and Colleen prayed. We told him that, not unlike the story of Shadrach, Meshach, and Abednego, where they were thrown into the fiery furnace, they came out the other side not even smelling like smoke. I would whisper that into Shane's ear every day. "You're going to come out not even smelling like smoke or arena dirt." We kept believing that.

Stacy Marquiss, my fellow cancer-surviving princess and Shiloh's and Shane's babysitter from their childhood, was living in Weatherford at the time, working two jobs and earning her teaching degree. She would bring her joy, agreement, and faith and would help anoint the essential oils almost every weekend. I think I was too emotional to do the raindrop with the oils.

Thankfully, Stacy, along with my niece Robin, would come at different times to anoint Shane with the oils. We were cautious but determined to help in every way we could. Lo and behold, we kept passing the little tests set by Dr. Warden.

I'll never forget the day she came in and said, "All right, Shane, we're moving up!" We were overjoyed, as it was the answer to the prayers we had been lifting since week one.

We were at least a month and a half in, and we thought that if we could just make it to Baylor Rehab in Dallas, we were going to get him better. I believed that when I was fighting for the insurance at JPS. I just knew if we could get him in an environment where his try could come into play, we were going to get him well. Preparation was made accordingly, and he was finally strong enough. We were taking Shane to the next level.

The passage to Baylor Rehab from the Select floor at Baylor Hospital was a tunnel underneath the city street that you could pass through on a gurney to the other side and into the rehab facility. You never even had to go outside. We celebrated and prayed over him, and though I cannot recall the exact words, I know we left everything behind, everything the enemy had come against us with—all the hardship, all the setbacks. We spoke into existence the healing that only God could provide, not unlike Him speaking all existence into being. *Let there be light*, the Scripture says, and we had light! We spoke it into being!

We were leaving all those obstacles from the past in the pit of hell with satan where they belong, at the bottom of that tunnel, at the lowest point. And when we were coming up the other side, we would start the complete healing process and continue the miraculous proof of the promises that God provides. He wants us well. We didn't look back, only up.

> *"Not that I have already attained, or am already perfected; but I press on, that I may lay hold of that for which Christ Jesus has also laid hold of me. Brethren, I do not count myself to have apprehended; but one thing I do, forgetting those things which are behind and reaching forward to those things which are ahead. I press toward the goal for the prize of the upward call of God in Christ Jesus."*
> **—Philippians 3:12-14**

We serve a God that can do more than we could ever imagine. We could only improve, just like ascending up out of that tunnel. It was glorious to see it play out that way. Dr. Dubiel at Baylor Rehab was the most beautiful, precious, faith-filled and positive force besides Kathee that we'd seen yet. Her staff and every physical therapy, occupational therapy, educational, and speech person in the building were so uplifting. Shane, like every man, was enticed by his beautiful doctor and would work harder to perform all that was asked to keep her happy. It helped that she was faith-filled, caring, and encouraging, and we loved the entire team that we had, including the care of the nurses who helped him get strong in his room to set him up for success.

SARAH PRIOLEAU'S LETTER

As a nurse, you have patients that change your career. Shane, to this date, is still the most remarkable and memorable patient I ever had the privilege to take care of.

Shane's parents spent every day at his bedside. Night and day. Advocating for him. Praying over him. Never doubting that he would recover, even despite the delivery of bad news, scans, and labs. They always saw the positive in the negative. Their faith and hope during a dark time were and still are so inspiring to me. A parent's love for their child is so healing in itself. I think this was a huge contributing factor to his recovery.

I had taken care of Shane many nights, but this night was different. I went in for my routine neurological exam around 4 a.m. Up until that point, Shane had only postured or withdrew to painful stimuli. This was indicative of the severe DAI he had suffered. On this day, he squeezed my hand immediately when I asked. I was in shock, my own heart racing. I asked him again. And he squeezed my hand again. Shane's dad was at the bedside, sleeping on the tiny bench we had. He could hear in my voice the excitement and stood up to come to the bedside. I told him that Shane had just followed commands. I'm pretty sure that we both just cried. It was the sign we had all been waiting for. From that day forward, hope was high. We saw Shane make massive strides toward neurological recovery every single day.

Shane's recovery, above all, is proof of God. No medication, treatment, or therapy alone can explain how or why he woke up that day. Shane, we are

LOOK UP

all so impressed and proud of your journey and enjoy watching you continue to change lives. I know you forever changed mine.

(Note: *Sarah was our supportive and faith-filled nurse at the first hospital JPS and also our FuManChu [beard and mustache] artist. We will forever be grateful for her and all the phenomenal help that led to our next group of above-and-beyond medical staff.)*

Elsie and Cindy, his aides at Baylor, were unbelievable. Shane was starting to be present with us and remember because, to this day, he does not remember two weeks before the accident or two months afterward due to the state he had been in. We kept him alive through all the negative things spoken over him—the malfunctioning brain probe, the trouble with his trach, the misplaced feeding tubes. We got him through the abscess surgery and the infection it caused. He passed the Warden's test, and he reached a point where he could start rehabbing his body and his brain communicatively. Watching God answer our prayers in real time gave us plenty to send in the Praise Report. We are starting to look for our shades because we saw a bright future!

However, we also had to wait for that prayer that we prayed at the beginning: complete healing. It was too early to claim victory over the war because we had so much battling left to do, but we knew that God is faithful and that He had stayed with us to this point and would continue. We gave God the glory and the recognition, but the mission remained. We were ready to do all the things that allowed us to glorify God and what He could do if we only believed.

Hope was heightened as it followed the most arduous and toughest valley that we encountered to that point. Humor was critical to release the frustration, and it kept us from imploding. We laughed until we cried in hysteria when we realized that we were fussing at his defiance. We found ourselves telling him to be still and quit tossing pillows! So we celebrated instead. The battles call for many actions. We dug in and came up smiling, finally able to take a deep breath and long sigh for the first time since the accident. We were on our knees praising God and thanking Him, looking up because it was about to get better.

We were joy-filled because we made it to Baylor Rehab, which, in the beginning, no one thought was possible. We finally felt like we were over the hump, that we made it and were going to get him better. Nobody thought he'd ever see it. That said, Shane was still weak. He was fully supported by a wheelchair. Thankfully, the point of Baylor Rehab was to get him better, and they were the most hopeful field we'd seen so far. They expected recovery, too. They were more cautious in getting him to each next step, but we believed in miracles. We believed full steam that he would make a full recovery—no wheelchairs, nothing—and though there was no evidence to show it yet, it was time to put the athlete in him to work.

The one hiccup was that one OT (occupational therapist) got fired. If you only looked at Shane, you wouldn't think much progress had been made. However, his brain was already coming back, and he was pretty sharp and aware. He didn't do repetitive therapy. It was redundant to him. He accomplished tasks and was ready to move to the next step.

One day, Shane had a replacement occupational therapist because his original OT had broken her back. The replacement, however, spoke down to Shane which was offensive toward him. Shane, in charge of his own care, made it clear that she was not welcome, and she was promptly replaced.

The memo quickly spread: we were all there to support Shane, and his voice mattered. The staff took it in stride and brought in another therapist who was just as wonderful as the rest of the team.

There were no issues with the other therapists—speech, education, and beyond—they were all simply God-sent.

Pam, his speech therapist, called him a badass, and he called her a badass right back. It became their thing—whenever they passed each other in the hallway, they'd say, "Hey badass," with a grin.

His physical therapist, Cat, was an overachiever who, along with her helper, DeAnthony, worked tirelessly to hold him up and catch him if he fell. Cat was our "land girl," while Lorraine, his "pool girl," brought her years of experience in water therapy. The two therapists had a friendly competition—if one could achieve something on land, the other would try to top it in the water, and vice versa.

This fabulous rivalry was the perfect way to motivate Shane, a hardworking cowboy athlete who already understood the value of effort and determination. Cat even coined the nickname "Rockstar" for Shane, as he consistently went above and beyond in every single therapy session, pushing himself to exceed expectations.

Shane was no different with another one of his overachieving therapists, Andrea. She was just as competitive as the rest of us. She and Shane laughed and competed and when he beat her, it was legit. She was not giving him one bit of mercy. And with as much smack talk he was communicating, she shouldn't have! It was fun to watch that team take Shane and bring him back to the Shane we recognized. It was healing for us to see him laughing and joking because he was so serious about getting well; it was good to give him purpose. He needed that purpose to keep discouragement at bay because he was so emancipated. None of this came until hours and days of therapy and the raindrop sessions of all those oils that Stacy, Robin, and I had been anointing on him from the beginning. God was with us in that place.

We placed Shane on the gym floor for the first time, using wedges and a towel rolled up under his forehead to give him room to breathe. We were so grateful to have found an inventive way to avoid smothering him while applying oils to his spine. Shane couldn't assist us at all during those sessions, but each time, he gained something—whether it was movement or strength. We knew the oils were just one of many vital components in Shane's recovery, and we used them faithfully.

It was during this time that Shane truly earned the name *Rockstar Cowboy*. Everyone at the facility began to call him that, and the nickname even made it into the *Praise Reports*.

There were sweet and amazing people—strangers to us—who had been at the rodeo and witnessed the accident. One such family, the Hatchers, understood brain injury; the mother had been in a car wreck. She and her two beautiful daughters came to Baylor Rehab and brought Shane a t-shirt featuring a steer wrestler with the words *Rockstar Cowboy*.

So many people, even those who didn't know us, reached out to pray for Shane. By then, we were well into day one-hundred-and-something, and yet strangers still had faith that Shane would recover. The road ahead was still long, but we were finally moving forward.

Faith-filled, we hit our stride. Hallelujah, people believed in our boy's recovery. They began to see our faith in action—in real time. We counted on it, believed it, pushed for it, planned for it, and worked tirelessly to make it happen.

> "For as the body without the spirit is dead,
> so faith without works is dead also."
> **—James 2:26**

Mushy Monday brought a visit from Robin, our constant reminder that Shane was fully present. Those baby blues of his locked onto her gaze with gratitude as he stood independently in the pool. He walked across the pool to her and gave her a kiss. I captured that moment on film—one of the very few photos we allowed of Shane during this time, given how thin and weak he was. In this picture, you could see the love in his eyes, a love he effortlessly shared with everyone he met, letting them know he truly saw them.

If that moment wasn't priceless enough, the crescendo came when Shane climbed the seven steps out of the pool and sat down on the bench at the top.

Cheers erupted from everyone in the pool area, echoing throughout the space. It sounded like Shane had just won the first round at Cheyenne, which, coincidentally, was happening at the time. There wasn't a dry eye in the place.

Glory! It was a beautiful sight.

Not to be outdone, Lorraine—affectionately nicknamed *Lorraine From The Plain*—kicked things up a notch the next day because of her playful competition with Kat, the physical therapist. Fueling the effort, Shane had climbed up and over the steps during land therapy, holding onto the rail. It was a breathtaking moment for all of us—nobody was holding onto him. We had been waiting for him to be strong enough to do that and with their competition even more!

Calls from cowboys at the *Daddy of 'em All* brought encouragement, and Shane's therapy milestones gave him good news to share. It was the much-needed push to keep him motivated and encouraged—staying in the boogie!

> *"He has made everything beautiful in its time. Also He has put eternity in their hearts, except that no one can find out the work that God does from beginning to end."*
> **—Ecclesiastes 3:11 NKJV**

We had Robin and Lee Ann Rust, the teacher of all the horse bodywork Shane had learned. I've known Lee Ann my entire life—she's tougher than anyone I've ever met. They came on different days of the week, each offering their unique help. None of us stopped watching Shane as he improved during those four hours of therapy each day.

One of the therapies he mastered was the Ekso bionic suit, which literally stood him up and helped him walk. Shane progressed so much that he could handle more than four hours of therapy a day. As a result, the team was preparing to send him to the next phase of his recovery, and we had to start preparing ourselves for that transition. By then, we were pretty attached to our team, constantly joking and building bonds like family.

I remember one particular day vividly. Shane was pushing his limits, doing things far beyond his current capabilities. By the end of the day, four different people had told him seven different times they were going to "kick his butt" for doing dangerous things that could have caused further injury.

I thought to myself, *Pam might call you a badass, but your momma is about to kick your ass if you don't knock it off!* And so, I told him!

The team was always trying to keep Shane safe; they didn't want any setbacks, and it was their job to enforce limits. The camaraderie and ease among everyone were so wonderful to witness. Meanwhile, Shane would just laugh—this full-body, shaking, giggling laugh—because if he managed to get a rise out of us, he felt like he was in control of the situation.

Early on at Baylor Rehab, Momma Nancy McCain—the lead angel of *Operation Wyoming Rescue*—got Shane a tablet to help him communicate, as speech was still a challenge. Nancy is notorious for being an angel to many. It was a delight that my childhood friend, Gary Don McCain, would choose such a wonderful addition to our "tribe" as his bride, and both have been an irreplaceable blessing in my life. Gary Don and I are so close that he was a pallbearer at my mother's funeral.

Nancy loved watching Shane's progress, especially the steps he took in the amazing Ekso bionic suit. Nancy stayed by his side, patiently waiting for more irreplaceable blessings to unfold—one of which was his first outing in a wheelchair.

And where did Nancy spoil him, you may ask? At none other than Del Frisco's famous steakhouse in Fort Worth, where Stacy just happened to be working at the time. Nancy and Gary Don, being family chosen decades ago, helped us revel in Shane's delight of good food with an outstanding dessert to top it off to add to that special outing.

Shane was getting away with a bit of what he wanted, even while pushing the limits of what the team allowed. Despite this, the team adored our newly-named *Rockstar* and celebrated his remarkable progress. However, Shane had improved too much to stay at Baylor any longer, so we began searching for the next best facility to continue his recovery journey.

Jim and I visited several places we believed would suit Shane's needs. While we explored our options, Shane's childhood friend Katie Hedeman and Momma Cindy Hedeman took on the full-time job of keeping our wild man safe from his antics.

On the surface, the Centre for Neuro Skills seemed like the best choice.

We were sad to say goodbye to the fun and supportive bunch at Baylor, but we knew it was time to move on.

We kept looking upward, knowing that great things awaited—even though challenges inevitably came with every new place. As long as we stayed in forward motion, we would make our way toward the possible. We were, and will remain, believers.

STACY MARQUIS'S LETTER

The moment that I read Trina's post that Shane had been hurt and was being Careflighted to Fort Worth, my heart sank. This was the young, charming, extremely loveable kid that I've known his whole life. I got to JPS on Mother's Day to check in on my friend and to get the update on Shane. They let me go back to see him, and it was a feeling I'll never forget. He looked so helpless in his unconscious state, and I was begging God to use me to help him. I immediately dug into my essential oils and talked to every "oil savvy" person that I knew to put together a plan to help save his brain. Trina and I stood firm in our agreement that Jesus would restore him completely. I truly believe to this day that the mass amounts of oils that we slathered on the bottoms of his feet day after day saved his brain.

When he was moved to Select, the nightmare of the infection with the feeding tube contributed to him dropping weight like no other. This young man made of muscle was withering away. It all seemed so grim, but we didn't weaken in our faith. We talked, we prayed, we spoke life over him, and we weren't accepting mediocre. Full restoration! I remember when he was awake and looking at us, but not really there. It was terrifying to see our person like this and not know how this was all going to play out. I recall the first time they put him on the swinging table thing, strapped in from chest to ankles so that he could stand upright. It was a major step and we knew that we had to keep speaking life and healing every single day.

I was with Jim and Trina the day that Shane made the move from Select to Baylor. I recall packing up the room that we'd spent so much time relying on faith that he was headed for the next step in his healing. We'd noticed all of the things that he couldn't do, like move his left arm, but we had faith that he would regain all of those abilities with time, healing aids, and Jesus. They wheeled him out in his bed, and we began the journey to his new temporary home. As the nurses pushed him in his bed through the tunnel, Trina and I were behind him, praying and so hopeful. I remember our arms stretched out to Jesus as we hit the bottom of the tunnel and the glory that we felt going up the hill toward the brain unit. The feeling that Jesus was walking right there with us and standing in agreement with us that Shane would be healed. When the doctors did all of their assessments of him that day, I was standing at the foot of his bed when they told him how much he weighed. Shane looked at me like a deer in the headlights with the reality of how much weight (about 60 pounds) he'd actually lost up to that point. I knew that he was cognitively there, even though he couldn't speak to us yet. We charged on with prayer, love, and a lot of oils!

Not too long after moving to Baylor, we decided it was time to try to do a raindrop on him to get things moving. It was hard to move him because he had no control of his body, and we were literally maneuvering dead weight. We went to the physical therapy room and proceeded to get him on the table, laying face down so that I could do the raindrop. He couldn't hold his own head up and we had to position him so that he could breathe. This was definitely not an easy task, but we got it done.

After every raindrop treatment, we saw something new come back to life or begin to move. We praised Jesus with each tiny improvement that we experienced. Little by little, he gained ground. Still not talking, I recall a therapist pointing at me and asking him who I was. He mouthed, "Stacy Marquiss." The joy I felt was indescribable. He not only knew who I was, but my first and last name. We knew he was all there and it would just take more time until he could talk to us. We slowly began doing new things, going downstairs to church on Sunday mornings, and I remember the first time he had pizza sitting in the eating area at Baylor. His hand was shaking so bad that it was difficult to get the pizza to his mouth, and he had it all over himself, but we laughed and were joyful that he was making such strides. He was even waking up in the night and stealing the snacks and honeybuns that were stashed in his room. The humor of the old Shane was beginning to return, and we were so thankful. He thought he was stronger than he was at that point, and we nearly lost him in a crash when he tried to go from the bed to the chair by himself without assistance. Not good Shane, not good!

Still in college and driving back and forth to Dallas every weekend, I did it because the Hadleys have always been a second family to me. I knew the oils and the prayers were working, and we just had to keep going. Keep making strides and keep seeing results. Faith does amazing things, and the miracle that we witnessed will forever be with me. Trina and I stood on firm ground in agreement from day one that he would be restored, and he was. Shane works every day to get better and heal. He's had some really high highs, and some really low lows. His faith in Jesus has carried him through so much and continues to be his rock in times of uncertainty. We give all glory to God for saving Shane's life that day on the arena floor, and I look forward to seeing all of the great things he will accomplish and the lives that he'll touch.

CHAPTER 6

I SEE YOU

"And my God shall supply all your need according to His riches in glory by Christ Jesus. Now to our God and Father be glory forever and ever. Amen."
—Philippians 4:19-20 NKJV

Moving Shane into the next rehab facility was definitely a "Nancy thing." Early on, she had a gift for helping him learn to be self-sufficient in certain ways. At the Centre for Neuro Skills (CNS), she made his room both motivational and homey, creating an environment that inspired him to keep pushing forward.

CNS offered an inpatient program where patients lived in an apartment with a roommate and caretakers. They were then bussed to the facility for six hours of therapy each day. However, there was one non-negotiable for us: we weren't going to leave Shane alone.

It was the absolute best decision we made. We hadn't left his side up to that point, and we weren't about to start until he was ready to come home. Although Shane had made incredible progress, he still wasn't well enough to stay the course without us ensuring he avoided being swept into the system's standard of "just good enough." We never settled for good enough. We were searching for something far beyond the ordinary. Unfortunately, in a high-volume setting, excellence is often compromised in the effort to manage such a large number of patients in need. To meet the demands of volume, it seems they focus primarily on teaching patients how to function, how to get along, and how to meet their basic needs—ensuring they are not a burden to themselves or those around them.

When you're truly aiming for complete recovery, you don't just think about functioning—you strive to thrive. You focus on an individualized workout plan tailored to specific needs, not a one-size-fits-all approach. Then, you prepare to take the next step in the progression.

We didn't fit the cookie-cutter model. The expectation was for Shane to come home after six hours of therapy—plus additional sessions—heat up a processed microwave meal, and do his laundry as the ultimate goal. But his goals were purposeful, designed to take him to the next level. At that stage, eating processed food wasn't an option and doing laundry wasn't the greatest priority—there were more vital things to be achieved in a specific sequence.

We have some friends—the Merritts from Wyoming—whose kids rodeo with our kids. Joann Merritt, a dear, handy cowgirl friend and fellow cancer survivor, called me one night, and during a rare moment of vulnerability, I confessed my struggles with the dining situation. Knowing my complete lack of culinary enthusiasm, she understood the challenge I was facing. I have a sign in my kitchen that reads, *"I have a kitchen because it came with the house."* My husband, on the other hand, is a phenomenal cook. Before we married, he had been a bachelor who enjoyed cooking, inspired by his grandfather. He takes great pride in his talent and is incredibly skilled in many areas—especially as a walking encyclopedia on history and other topics.

I've always been happy to trade kitchen duties for any ranch chores or domestic responsibilities to avoid the pressure of meal preparation. But by this point, Jim and I were taking shifts with Shane 24/7, and I didn't share his confidence in the kitchen.

Thankfully, Joann stepped in with a solution. She sent 30-minute meal kits using HelloFresh boxes, which were a lifesaver. With their step-by-step instructions, I could make gourmet meals that gave the illusion I could cook! Shane was eating nutritious meals, and the quick prep time allowed us to get him showered and resting without delay.

Meanwhile, I found myself constantly battling with CNS staff members, many of whom were new hires with limited English proficiency. These staff members were assigned to oversee patients in their apartments, but the language barrier often led to misunderstandings. One incident involved an inexperienced worker who insisted on waking Shane up to make him use the bathroom—a completely unnecessary and counterproductive action for a brain injury patient.

I refused to let that happen. Sleep is critical for brain healing, and Shane needed rest more than anything. I stood my ground, arguing until I was forced to call management to intervene before the cowgirl in me handled it differently! The idea of waking a groggy, brain-injured patient to check an unnecessary box was absurd. Shane knew when he needed to go, and we were there to help him—not to force him into a routine that didn't serve his recovery.

This wasn't an isolated issue. New staff members often approached Shane with a checklist of tasks, asking him to perform unnecessary tests like stating his name, the date, or who the president was. Shane had already spent more than the required six hours a day in therapy, pushing himself to his limits in every aspect. The patient's immediate needs were addressed with common sense and handled accordingly. When the brain is tired, it isn't like a muscle anyone can power through—it simply shuts down. It needs rest and rebooting.

To avoid these pointless exercises, I'd take their papers and quickly ask Shane a few questions myself. He would respond accurately, proving there was no need to test him further. It wasn't about defying staff; it was about respecting the patients and bringing new staff members up to speed immediately. Shane found it frustrating because he knew all that information, and again, doing repetitive things was an anger trigger. What he needed was therapy that helped him walk better, talk better, and function as a healed human being—not time-wasting tasks that served no purpose other than angering the patient and benefiting someone besides the patient. It reminded me of when Shane fired his occupational therapist at Baylor Rehab. He knew exactly what he needed—and what he didn't.

To that point in the healing process, Shane had progressed from being unable to hold his head up or speak to now being able to move from lying down to sitting, aiding in his transfer to a wheelchair, and communicating softly and minimally. The most basic functions were hard work. Showering and eating without falling or spilling were met with a goal-type mentality.

At the apartment, there was constantly one challenge or another. He would be so early to his bus to the clinic that, in the beginning, he would insist on wheeling himself down from one of the farthest apartments at the facility to get in the van and travel to where all the therapy was done. In the summer, he sat in his wheelchair, strapped in the van, sweating profusely while waiting on everybody else. We let that happen a couple of times before we chose to adjust the treatment schedule to best fit Shane. We drove him to the clinic ourselves, allowing him to stay after and work longer almost every day. At the clinic, we had an occupational therapist named Ligia, who made it possible to incorporate a hyperbaric oxygen chamber.

That specific therapy was made possible by longtime Wyoming rodeo/ranching family friends, the Scotts, who have been a big part of our everyday lives. When our kids were very little, Shane often found himself the lone boy in a "bathtub of estrogen," surrounded by four girls, including his sister, after many dusty ropings. He became the honorary brother to the three Scott girls and their two girl cousins, who often treated him as their own.

Spending time with them didn't soften him—after all, as they say, "Some of Wyoming's best cowboys are cowgirls." Tougher than most grown men, the girls helped keep Shane in line. So much so that during his freshman year, when their daughter Kelsey was a senior, Shane escorted her to cowboy prom at the state high school rodeo finals.

Shortly after I made it back to our hotel room, Shane returned. Concerned, we asked if something was wrong. "No," he replied.

We asked if he had a good time.

"Yes," he said.

Then why was he back so soon? Kelsey explained that they needed to get up early to rope and that Kelsey wanted them to get some rest.

Shane was never short on strong women in his life, between me, his sister, his cousins, and his friends. And when Shane got hurt, guess who was the first in line to help? The Scott family.

From afar, they started a GoFundMe campaign, raising a significant amount of money. Knowing the benefits of oxygen chambers firsthand, they decided to purchase one for Shane and have it sent to him! Kelsey had suffered multiple concussions while playing college basketball and other sports and had learned, with the help of the rodeo world, just how effective oxygen therapy could be.

The Scotts' generosity was matched by the support of our in-house team and, most importantly, our occupational therapist, Ligia, who helped us secure a special room for the chamber. Though the facility didn't provide oxygen therapy, she found a way to make it happen.

Each morning, we'd take Shane by car, set him up in the oxygen chamber for an hour before therapy, and then he'd tackle his six-plus hours of rehab, pushing himself to the limit. After staying later than the rest of the patients, we'd bring him home, whip up a 30-minute meal, shower, rest, and start all over again the next day.

Although Shane was still in a wheelchair, he stayed late to continue to work to get out of that wheelchair faster whenever he could. This facility worked for us because of the incredible support system that came together to make it happen. We were deeply grateful for everyone who contributed to Shane's recovery, especially the Scott family and rodeo friends, with their extraordinary gift.

While that was happening, the McCain family and another childhood friend, Shane Smith, helped set up the apartment in the city and kept us connected to home. Nancy was the interior decorator. She made sure Shane's room felt like his room, with inspirational items and pictures reminding him of home.

All of us were looking up again. Our attitude reflected nothing but faith in Jesus and the belief that Shane was getting better. The help continued when we returned to the city. Either Jim or I stayed with Shane, while the support from our friends in Stephenville and across the nation remained beyond humbling.

How could we ever repay the kindness and dedication of Dennis and Shan Motes, who watched over our place and cared for our animals for months during a drought year? Their care was the only reason we could be away for so long. Feeding our five horses twice daily in such dry conditions for months was an unpayable act of generosity. Although they would never call it a burden, Jim and I trading off weeks with Shane allowed us to finally relieve them of that responsibility.

While there were stressors, our new team brought fresh hope! Ligia, Shane's new occupational therapist, and Katie, his new physical therapist, were both incredible. They developed a strong bond with Shane, and he became especially close to each of them. So close, in fact, that he kept one of Katie's biggest secrets—her pregnancy. He could still keep a secret like he always had been able to do, and even now, when she needed someone to confide in. Later, when they shared the news with me, we all had a good laugh at how well he managed to keep secrets—it was truly on par with his skill in doing so!

That just goes to show how close Shane was with his therapists. Not everyone had that kind of bond, but Ligia was no exception when it came to Shane. Taken off course by his tomfoolery at times, she still admired his work ethic and strong will, crediting those qualities as key to his recovery. She also emphasized how essential our family's support was to his progress. Ligia acknowledged that our advocacy for Shane when he couldn't speak for himself was a beautiful and critical part of the progress he made.

She witnessed, as she put it, continual hope, love, and care from the family and friends who poured into Shane's recovery. As a believer herself, Ligia agreed that God was certainly in the midst of it all and that His work with Shane wasn't finished yet.

Everyone who came into Shane's room felt the presence of God and the Holy Spirit. People of faith are way-makers, and Ligia exemplified that by finding a spot for the oxygen chamber within the clinic. Since oxygen therapy wasn't available in-house, her solution ensured we didn't have to wait until Shane was back home to begin using it. Ligia's ability to secure a space that no executive could argue with went above and beyond her job description, but she made it happen.

The God moment in all of this was that Ligia wasn't even supposed to be Shane's occupational therapist. The therapist originally assigned to him came to Ligia somewhat panicked after reading in Shane's records that he had fired his occupational therapist at Baylor. She admitted she didn't know if she could handle him.

Ligia already had a full caseload of patients, but, true to her fearless nature, she took Shane on being the overachiever that she is and thinking to herself, *This cowboy, well, he isn't going to fire me!* She wasn't scared, and we absolutely loved that about her! She became his best advocate and greatest challenger. "I see you, 51," she'd say often, reminding him to rein in his impatience when it made him dangerous.

Ligia was the best at pushing Shane to stay compliant and focused. In occupational therapy, the little things mattered, and Shane couldn't rely solely on being the big, strong athlete—Ligia was all about the details. She was truly special and made the entire process smoother. Shane even went above and beyond for her, helping Ligia serve at the food pantry.

Her impact was matched by Katie and many other amazing therapists. The speech and education teams also had high expectations for Shane, often challenging him to make use of his business degree from Tarleton. "Come on, show me your business degree," they'd say, pushing him to excel in class, which he did. He worked so hard that he could afford to miss a day occasionally and spend extra time on areas where he struggled most.

The physical therapy team let Shane stay twice as long, giving him extra time to practice walking and pushing himself further. This dedication helped him power through those endless therapy days.

We give immense credit to the Scott family and our Wyoming ranch and rodeo community, who showed up to support us and demonstrated what was possible after their daughter's traumatic brain injury from college sports. Thanks to Jill Cde Baca's *One Hit Away Foundation*, we had a list of therapies to try, including oils and oxygen therapy. We researched and fully understood how all the "outside the box" therapies, oils, and oxygen worked together, and none of us, including Shane, were satisfied with simply achieving the status quo.

He did everything he could to heal his brain injury, driven not only by the exceptional staff but also by the unwavering support of the rodeo world.

> *"Two are better than one, because they have a good reward for their labor. For if they fall, one will lift up his companion. But woe to him who is alone when he falls, For he has no one to help him up."*
> —Ecclesiastes 4:9-10 NKJV

Sunil was an overachiever, too. He was one of the physical therapists who had been promoted and moved on, but he returned to the facility just to help Shane. Shane's *Rockstar Cowboy* nickname was well-earned and continued to define him at CNS. He kept working hard and putting in the effort, the same determination he showed at Baylor that earned him the nickname. That drive sustained him without a shred of doubt.

The hardships at the CNS apartment gradually lessened as we gained more control over our home environment. No one could force us to adhere to robotic checklists because we understood that focusing on foundational progress—not just the functional, survival-based goals they emphasized—would lead to better outcomes. With a different attitude, we were able to achieve much more.

In hindsight, the tasks Shane didn't do at CNS—laundry, cleaning, and cooking—weren't ignored; they were intentionally prioritized. He would later go above and beyond to make up for them, but at the time, the focus on his recovery enabled him to eventually handle those responsibilities—and much more—even more efficiently than expected. God's restoration functions in specific and seasonal times, which is not unlike our expectations. Get control of the body, and the chores will be done on a higher functioning level, which Shane's recovery would come to prove.

I didn't let him cook at the time because he was dangerous with the tremors in his left hand, and he had no business cutting things up. It took some time, but he now has a safe utensil that he uses in instances that require cutting things efficiently. Shane often cooks breakfast for his nieces and nephews with no aid at ease. We wanted him well for a lifetime of success.

You couldn't prove that their formula was the only way to heal him. He was doing 10 times more than what they were asking of him, going above and beyond just the basics. I'm so glad that God and the Holy Spirit pushed us to keep advocating against processes that didn't make sense. Just because it was protocol didn't mean we had to be ashamed of pursuing a path that was our own.

God made it so special by saving this child so miraculously. The comeback and the therapies used had to fit the same miraculous level and realm that we're walking in. And the thing is, when you do believe in the God that saves and you don't handcuff Him with your disbelief of what your human mind thinks He is capable of doing—go ahead and read what He can do. Those things and those promises that are written down in that Word are to see and speak into our own lives. Stand on, believe in, and thank Jesus for what could happen.

Great outcomes don't happen without action. The only things that God can't do for us are things that we're supposed to do for ourselves. I've said it before: if there's no action behind faith, then I'm all talk and no walk. But if we can get up each day and say, "Show me, use me, God," then we can stand on His promises, trusting and believing in them. Only then can I prove that I'm useful to God.

If I simply ask you to pray for me but don't take any action myself, then I'm only testing God—and we are commanded not to do that. When satan tempted Jesus by saying, "Go ahead and jump off; the angels will catch you," Jesus didn't test God. And why would He? Just to prove something to satan?

There was another time when an evil whisper from satan tempted a man, saying, "If you'll just stop breathing, I've got you." But if the man believed that lie and stopped breathing, he would die. God's name, *Yahweh*, is in our very breath because breath is life. Every breath we take proclaims His name. He gives us life.

At CNS, we were in a rough and scary part of the city. By that point, I was tired—really tired. I'd been taken advantage of too many times and had grown quite salty from the constant advocacy. One night, I remember pulling into a gas station, knowing I shouldn't be fueling up at that hour. But I have my license to carry, and I know how to use my weapon. I had taken gun safety classes, passed the tests, and knew how to shoot not only for protection but also skill for harvesting food or dealing with varmints on the ranch. Accuracy tested would best describe my aim.

A man pulled up and tried to intimidate me (using tactics I won't detail here), to make me feel unsafe, and to question whether I was in danger and in need of defending myself. After fighting for my son's life, I developed a fearlessness. I took my pistol, placed it on the dashboard—never removing my hand from it—and looked him straight in the eye. *Go ahead. Try me. You have no idea what this crazy white momma has been battling, and I have no problem defending myself.*

At that point, I was ready to fight a red-eyed lion. When you're that deep in a battle, you get that salty. The man saw my unshaken resolve, turned his music down, got in his car, and drove away. Immediately after, I felt a wave of reality hit me, and I asked God to reel me in. Maybe that wasn't the right way to handle the situation, no matter how dangerous it felt. Even when you're ready to protect yourself, you still have to operate from the love of God.

In my classes, I was taught to stay focused on the mission when I felt my life was in danger. I didn't act out of intimidation—I acted because I genuinely felt threatened and believed it was up to me to do something. Still, I realized I needed to approach even moments of fear with grace and trust in God's guidance.

Moments like that exemplify the things beyond the brain injury we were battling. Since that part of the Metroplex was one of the roughest areas, I didn't do it out of false fear, if you will. It was done because the Scriptures say we battle with things in the spiritual realm. Whatever was troubling that gentleman was being used against me as a way to instill fear. My duty is to respond with truth as a child of the Most High God: *"Thou shalt not fear."* The enemy will try to battle against you, but with Jesus in the mix, he must flee. No matter which direction the attack came from, we refused to let discouragement overtake us—then or at the next CNS facility. We stood on God's promises, His glory, and we didn't stop for good enough—not in the beginning, not in the middle, and not in the end.

There was one aide at CNS who came and stayed with us one night in the apartment. We prayed to have her whenever she was available. Her name was Kabita, and she would help Shane do therapy at home and help him with sign language when he still wasn't speaking very well so he wouldn't get frustrated. When Kabita was there, I knew I could take a break and that together, they would handle Shane's designed routine with ease.

It's so beautiful to celebrate those who want to work unto God, those who don't try to impress anybody but the excellence of God Himself. That's why we, as humans, seek that. When we have a connection and a love for God as He has love for us, we seek to be excellent where He is excellent. The inner motivation is why you work harder when nobody's looking. You do what's right when nobody's around, and you repent and apologize when you don't. Be successful enough and secure enough in your own choices that you can do that boldly and in confidence with one another without ever, ever having insecurity make you do otherwise. Staying in prayer helps that small, quiet, peace-filled voice guide confident, definitive choices.

Appreciating the progress made at CNS was the key to improving. Hope's light kept shining in the darkness and kept pushing Shane to get better, do better, and be better.

We don't know how we could have done it without all the extra help from friends, family, and our rodeo family, and we remain forever grateful. By this time, the Justin Cowboy Crisis Fund had been assisting Shane by covering any excess expenses and modalities he needed. The *One Hit Away Foundation*, guided by Jill's unwavering support, along with the various fundraisers held for Shane, brought us to our knees in gratitude and thanksgiving.

Our friends in Stephenville, together with our church and community, organized a benefit team roping event called *Send It For Shane*. Our neighbors and rodeo friends/champions, Brad and Barrie Smith, produced a phenomenal event. It rained that day, but our friends and neighbors worked tirelessly to make it a success. They compiled high-quality auction items donated from across the country, with contributions extending far beyond the Stephenville area, thanks to the vast reach of the rodeo world. Even more world champions like California steer wrestler John W. Jones and his son-in-law, Super Bowl-winning football player and steer wrestler Bear Pascoe, lent their support. World Champions and NFR Qualifiers too numerous to list, aided in this act that goes beyond generosity.

Though the turnout was smaller due to the rain, the event was held under the beautiful covered arena at the home of Randy and Teresa Quarne, who graciously hosted the round-robin team roping. Most of the Smith family and Shane's former employer poured their creativity into making the event a success. The team even took bids online and over the phone, ensuring that no one missed the chance to participate despite the weather.

By the end of the day, the event raised an incredible $50,000! This generosity made a huge difference, helping cover medical expenses like the helicopter and other costs that could have set Shane back.

LOOK UP

"Look at the birds of the air, for they neither sow or reap nor gather into barns; yet your heavenly Father feeds them. Are you not of more value than they?"
—Matthew 6:26 NKJV

Totally astonished by the love of our friends, family, and rodeo family, we couldn't stop praising the blessings chasing us down. Things were looking up because our support lifted us up. The rodeo, ranching, and western world know how to care for something other than themselves because of the life they live and their care for animals. People are worth more than birds. God will use anyone who's willing to be His physical hands and feet.

Cowboys raised in that environment definitely know how to support their loved ones—and even strangers they've never met. That was Shane's story. There were people who helped who had never even met him. They just knew they wanted to champion what God had started. Mark Anderson's Clinic with Jill Hansen and Russell Weise was another one of the fundraisers that went on, and we were blessed by events related to equine. The sole reason Jim and I were able to stay with Shane and advocate and supply him with so many extra modalities was due to all the collective rallying by everyone. Strangers to Shane's past employer, family, friends, and others' support, together, the roping, the donations, all the showerings of blessings - they were why we could be with him.

But as we celebrated all of the good, he was still really hurt.

His right arm still wasn't functional, and his tremors were severe in his left hand. He was especially dangerous with liquids, so we had to thicken his water to prevent choking. Hot drinks and sharp objects required extra caution as well. Shane was beginning to show signs of frustration and impatience—which, frankly, wasn't surprising.

We could empathize with the annoyances of being in a wheelchair, though not with sympathy—it lacked purpose. What we needed was a change.

Lo and behold, Lee Ann Rust, an old family friend, Shane's friend and former instructor in horse bodywork, walked in one day and said, "I think hippotherapy will help." This is a physical therapy treatment strategy that uses equine movement. The posture, balance, coordination, strength, and sensorimotor systems of the rider are affected by being on the horse through the rhythmic, three-dimensional movement, improving flexibility and overall functionality.

We already knew how transformative riding could be for a person.

After all, the saying holds true: "The outside of a horse is good for the inside of a man." Hippotherapy could be yet another equine blessing! We knew that the riding was there since Shane had been that way since birth. We had spoken about it with that group.

Shane's fellow steer wrestlers on the pro circuit pitched in, as they were known to do. Collectively, they form the broadest and most big-hearted group—a true band of brothers. Of all the events, steer wrestling is the only event that takes two cowboys to pull off, but only one is paid the prize money. The hazer is known as the most thankless job in all events but is of the utmost importance in guiding and blocking the steer with precise timing and execution. The close bond formed may be due to the deep level of trust you build when asking someone to ride into battle with you. It's a trust born from facing a shared challenge—a helper who only earns a portion of the payment if the one wrestling the steer succeeds. Rodeo athletes have the advantage of making the competition stay where it lies, in the arena against the animal or in coordination with the animal, whichever is the case. Those honorable men are always there for each other, helping one another compete by hazing cattle, sharing horses, and even literally helping to beat each other in competition. There's no better example of sportsmanship than what exists in the rodeo world, and the steer wrestlers exemplify that constantly. May the whole world emulate their lead.

They rallied around Shane, donating items, sending money, and even gifting a leather jacket and a signed card from a big jackpot. They also sent countless encouraging messages. Yet, in Shane's presence, their pain for him was evident. It was hard for them to see him like that—not only as a sobering reminder of how dangerous their profession is but also as a potential distraction from their own competitions, which requires their full focus.

It's difficult for overachieving men to be around something they can't fix, and Shane was a living reminder of that. For Shane, watching steer wrestling was equally hard, as it reminded him of what he was missing. It was a sad and challenging dynamic for both sides. I could see it in all of them because I have witnessed how incredible their hearts are. They are an inspirational group of men. *They, too, see you 51.*

As time went on, it became harder for Shane to be around the sport, but he hadn't yet given it up. He still believed he would return, and there was no way I was going to take that dream away from him.

Did I want him to steer wrestle again? Did Jim? Did his sister? Did anyone? No. We selfishly didn't want to risk losing him to another accident. But it wasn't our hope to take away from Shane. If we hadn't given him hope while he was still healing, we would have been extinguishing it instead of nurturing it.

No matter how much earthly evidence you have to prove otherwise, do you feel you have the right to steal someone's hope—their right to abide by what God's Word says: *faith, hope, and love*?

> *"And now abide faith, hope, love, these three;*
> *but the greatest of these is love."*
> **—I Corinthians 13:13**

Love them enough to allow the abiding. The definition of *abide* is to endure without yielding, to wait, to accept without objection, to remain stable, and to bear patiently. That's what it means to abide in your faith, your hope, and, most importantly, in your love.

Let each "bridge to be crossed" be crossed when you reach it. Allow everyone the time to see and cross that bridge in their own way and in God's timing. Don't let hurt undo the progress that has been made. It's okay to shoot for the stars—how else will you fall among them? Why limit what God can do? Because we're not done yet.

I believe God reminds us: "*I know you've made your plans, but I will design your steps.*"

> *"A man's heart plans his way,*
> *But the Lord directs his steps."*
> **—Proverbs 16:9 NKJV**

I believe one reason Scripture exists is because sometimes we get ideas in our heads, thinking we've come up with the best plan. But, as Shane's story shows, God always has a better one. The plans we make before the wreck, before the trials, often pale in comparison to what God has in store. It's painful, it's hard to deal with, and it's difficult to admit. But if you have the strength to do so, you can rise up out of the arena dirt and say, "Okay, God, I trust You."

I know for a fact that Shane's story—being hurt and coming back—glorified God and showcased His miracles in more glorious ways than winning any championship ever could.

I respect and love the sport deeply, but the Bible reminds us that earthly prizes will fade. That's why we're called to store up our treasures in heaven, first, where they far outweigh anything this world can offer.

When you look at life through that lens and cling to God's promises—promises that extend to eternity—it puts everything else into perspective. Winning a rodeo event feels small in comparison. It's incredibly humbling.

> *"But lay up for yourselves treasures in heaven,*
> *where neither moth nor rust destroys and*
> *where thieves do not break in and steal."*
> **—Matthew 6:20 NKJV**

As much as we strive for excellence in the rodeo arena, don't you know He just laughs at us? Not because we're seeking His excellence or wanting to showcase the athleticism He's blessed us with—that brings Him joy. But He laughs when we put it ahead of Him, when we think it's more important than bringing others to know Him.

We couldn't help but believe that Shane's injury brought more attention to God than any arena win ever could. That's a hard truth to swallow when all you want is to be a champion. But it's also a sobering reminder of who we serve and where our priorities must lie.

We must put faith and evidence behind our beliefs. When things are tough, who or what do you turn to? What are your words saying? What do your actions reflect?

When life isn't going your way, when tragedy strikes, are you screaming at Him for help, or are you wasting precious time asking, "Why?" You don't need to wonder why—it's already been told to us. John 10:10 reminds us that until the second coming of Christ, the enemy roams the earth, seeking to steal, kill, and destroy. God can use anyone and anything for His good, yet the enemy will use *anyone* or *anything* **(thoughts, etc.)**, *willing* to fulfill the opposing way from God.

> *"The thief does not come except to steal, and to kill,*
> *and to destroy. I have come that they may have life,*
> *and that they may have it more abundantly."*
> **—John 10:10**

Jesus came so that we may have life into abundance and to the full. Knowing Jesus gives you guidance from His Holy Spirit. He left with us as a Helper in the present time. It's also okay to look forward to an eternity in heaven, knowing that in this life, you're just passing through. You can make it as glorious or as miserable as you choose—not based on your circumstances or the things that happen to you, but on the attitude you carry through it all.

When you adopt an attitude of, *Thank You, Lord. I know You're providing a way*, and then you have something to get excited about. But if you sit there saying, *Oh, Lord, I hope it's Your will,* you're essentially doubting Him. What you're really saying is that you need the Maker of the universe to prove Himself to you beyond what He's already written in His Word for your reassurance.

It's your responsibility to know His truth. God can't do for you what you can do for yourself. If you don't know what His Word says, of course, you'll question it. That's why, when the enemy comes to steal, kill, and destroy, you must take every thought captive, as the Bible instructs.

For instance, if you think, *Well, I just suck,* do you really believe that? Do you believe what God says about you? Because if you do, then you know you're *beautifully and wonderfully made* and the *apple of His eye*. It doesn't matter what others think of you—or even what you think of yourself. If you believe what God believes about you, you won't hold onto those negative thoughts about yourself or anyone else.

Instead, you'll receive His love, learn to love yourself, and become a river rather than a reservoir. You'll let His love flow through you to others. That's exactly what our therapists did. They gave of themselves to help each person rediscover who God created them to be.

When you live in that kind of care and surround yourself with people like those in the rodeo industry who freely give of themselves, it's no wonder they are so grounded in Christ. The Code of the West is rooted in biblical principles. I watched family, friends, and rodeo family members step in to help Shane in different ways—even if they couldn't be there physically.

We had to drive from the city, a couple of hours away, to participate in hippotherapy with Lee Ann. We were excited because the movement of a horse's steps mimics the motion of human hips. It is incredibly purposeful and was beneficial for our cowboy's mental game and physical recovery.

The first horse we were put on was so old and crippled. I think I felt more sorry for the horse than anything. We rushed Shane from the city. He was in shorts, mind you, in tennis shoes, a T-shirt, and a helmet. If he was going to get a horseback, he had to wear a helmet. It took two or three cowboys, Jim and me, to get him on the horse from his wheelchair. But when we did, the joy we saw was immediate. We knew we had something.

At the facility, you could only get 23-hour passes, or else insurance would consider you an outpatient and disqualify your care and treatment plan. We would bust a move out of the city of Irving, Texas and haul it down to Stephenville for therapy and then possibly go get a good night's rest. Sometimes, we would wheel into our Erath County Cowboy Church in Stephenville and then get back to Irving in 23 hours.

Shane was starting to get to sleep one night in his own bed. He was starting to be horseback. He was starting to see his church family. He was still in the wheelchair, but we were doing it. We were doing it.

Waiting in the wings was the epitome of a cowgirl, Barrie Smith, who had produced the *Send It For Shane* roping event. I told Barrie about a crippled horse we were doing therapy with and how hard it was to watch an animal hurting as much as a human. Barrie responded, "I've got a horse for Shane."

Before I knew it, we were using the very horse her son had ridden at the National Finals Rodeo in Las Vegas in calf roping. His name was Cowboy, and like most calf horses, he was reactive. But for Shane, Cowboy became the sweetest, most gentle, patient, and kind animal. He couldn't have taken better care of him.

At the very beginning, Barrie's son, Sterling, who had ridden Cowboy at the NFR, asked if she really thought Cowboy was the right horse for Shane. With her fingers crossed behind her back, Barrie replied, "Oh, it will be great."

Every hippotherapy session with Barrie felt like a level-up. Sterling's skepticism mirrored my own, but we trusted her cowgirl judgment. There were five of us—myself, Jim, Judah, Tori, and Barrie—and it took all five of us to get Shane on Cowboy. Once he was mounted, Cowboy plodded along, handling it all so well. It took months of those 23-hour passes and numerous trips down from the city to progress before he was able to go faster.

At first, we hand-walked Shane ourselves. Then Barrie began saddling her old horse, Richard, to ride alongside them. Richard wasn't the most laid-back horse; he was immensely talented in his own right and remained observant as usual. However, rather than being his typically antisocial self, he seemed to be acting out of care. When Shane came out of the truck off balance to get on Cowboy, Richard walked up, rested his head between Shane's shoulders, and nudged him along, keeping him from falling back. Miraculous and definitely out of Richard's character! After each ride, Richard would follow Shane down the steps, placing his forehead in the middle of Shane's back to help balance him.

We had never seen anything like it. Horses seem to know when you're hurt, meeting you where you are and helping you heal. It was amazing and unbelievable that the least likely horse to want to stand near a human was the one holding Shane up. If that's not a God moment and a testament to His creation, I don't know what is.

We were deeply moved that Shane could ride again. Eventually, Shane and Barrie progressed to riding outside the arena in the pasture. Shane grew a little cockier, sliding his weight and cocking down in the right stirrup like he was going to dismount onto a steer. He scared us all, then laughed his butt off as we hollered at him. His belly laugh was infectious.

Still, at a walk, it was pure joy, and we knew we were making progress since he was able to pull himself back up square in the saddle. That joy was healing, and every ride with Barrie was filled with laughter and hope. Barrie truly was the best medicine we found. After a session with her, Shane's staff could achieve so much more during in-house therapy.

We didn't miss a weekend of riding, as far as I can remember. Once, they were out in the pasture checking cows when Barrie's beloved Brahman cow, Creamer, came over for her cow cake. It's rare for a cow to approach a horse, but Creamer adored Barrie. Shane fed her cake from horseback, surrounded by the familiar smells of the ranch life he'd grown up with—a joy that brought healing.

The joy of the Lord was our strength. Hippotherapy became so purposeful that after those months of dedication, Shane progressed from walking to trotting, learning to control his legs to use the stirrups for balance. Barrie also incorporated all kinds of different arm movements during the rides. I'd ask, "What kind of therapy are you doing?"

They'd giggle and reply, "We don't know, but it's working."

Barrie and Shane were precious together. Though Barrie wasn't formally trained in hippotherapy, her expertise as a skilled cowgirl and her deep understanding of body structure and balance on a horse made her as effective as any professional therapist.

We continued by putting a rope in Shane's hand. At this point, Shane couldn't raise his arm much higher than his waist, so there was almost no clearance over Cowboy's head. We tried to have him swing the rope out beside Cowboy's head, but he couldn't manage it. Instead, he kept whacking Cowboy in the eye.

Most horses would shy away, maybe jump, move their head, or do something—but not Cowboy. He just stood there and took it, blinking his eye. Finally, we said, "Shane! You've got to stop. You have got to get some clearance. You're giving Cowboy a little too much abuse there!" When Shane stopped, Cowboy seemed visibly relieved, and we all giggled and carried on.

But again, that's *not* the nature of a calf horse. If Shane had been whacking Cowboy in the head while roping a calf in the practice pen or at the NFR, the horse would have reacted differently—backing up, moving away, or doing something to avoid the discomfort. The self-sacrificing nature of these animals, especially Cowboy, was phenomenal. It was enough to bring tears to your eyes.

Eventually, Shane managed to get a little clearance with his rope, improving bit by bit. He progressed to riding on his own, a significant milestone. Riding helped us all in ways I didn't fully realize at the time. I needed to get back on horseback, too—to feel connected again to everything we belonged to, rather than the concrete version of life we had been living.

Riding and roping had always been part of our daily lives, and we missed home deeply. We thanked God for all our horses and for Shane on Cowboy, who didn't mind being roped around the neck or even taking a few accidental hits. He just took it all in stride.

There was a time when Jim and I were gone, and Shane wanted to ride the few miles over to Barrie's. He went through the back pastures of the neighbors, where Barrie had to wait on him because it took him a while to open and shut all the gates in between our place and theirs. By the time he got to the ranch, he was so tired that Barrie's husband, Brad, had to load him up in the trailer to take him and his horse back, but he did, however, make the ride over. It was quite the accomplishment in itself and another beautiful moment spent getting better with Barrie. We now just need more clearance with his roping arm.

Lee Ann to the rescue. She brought in another guru from her department of expertise, a sports massage therapist, trained and licensed with both humans and horses, who had some unique techniques that other therapists might not have addressed. Her remarkable work was described as a pressure point release system. Melissa Martin-Luce (the licensed massage therapist) accommodatingly drove to Irving to meet Shane after hours after a therapy session and did her bodywork on him in the apartment at CNS.

MELISSA MARTIN'S LETTER

> *In 2018, I had a call from a mutual friend of the Hadleys and mine, LeeAnn Rust, who had spoken with me about the horrific steer wrestling accident that Shane Hadley was in. His mother, Trina, had called me and asked if I could come and evaluate Shane to see if there was anything I*

could do to help him. My mindset is always, absolutely! My intent is to do what's best for my client and make every client better than when I started.

Shane was in a wheelchair when I met him and his family. He and I had a tad bit of a communication problem due to his speech being slurred, although I had no problem understanding him when I hit trapped muscles and released them. Shane was contracted on his right side to the point he had to use his left hand to move his right hand across his torso. His body was on lockdown, trapping muscles, nerves, oxygen, internal organs, blood, and lymphatic flow. The restriction of oxygen to his entire body was limited from the ribcage not functioning to its fullest capacity.

The first objective of mine was to release the ribcage to get more oxygen to flow to his body and brain for more efficient healing. The second was to release the rotator cuff muscles, open the brachial plexus, and free up his biceps brachii muscles. I remember when I had finished Shane's shoulder release, we did some active and passive movement to allow his brain to acknowledge the freedom of movement and strength. Not a moment later, he reached over to grab his right hand with his left to move it, and I smacked his left hand. He gave me a curious glance as I told him to reach across his body with his right; it was slow, but he could do it. The last place that I thought I could help at that time was his balance and stability. Shanes' hips were rotated, one anteriorly and one posteriorly. At this time, his parents were describing the toning he would get periodically, which explained the extremely tight leg muscles I had to release—rotating his hips back to a neutral position, releasing the sacroiliac joints, and allowing the nerves to relax and inflammation to decrease. To say the least, this was a process and took time.

Around the third session, I mentioned to Jim and Trina about hippotherapy, which I thought would be beneficial to Shanes' recovery. Equestrians have a bond with horses that is like no other, and if nothing else, it would help with his psyche and improve his quality of life. I was not a part of the hippotherapy, but I heard some great stories about his sessions.
Shane improved by leaps and bounds; he was the miracle client and or patient to all his therapists. Quit was not in his vocabulary and he proved it on a daily basis.

I offered for Shane to come with me when I worked on horses. Since he had had experience doing it before, I thought it would be a continuation of semi-therapy and an opportunity for him to make a little money. The horses gravitated to him and received his touch willingly, with an understanding that they were truly helping each other.

*(**Note:** Melissa is a licensed sports massage therapist. Back in Balance is her business, and she also has equine therapy certification.)*

In just one session, he progressed from only being able to raise his hand to his waist to raising it above his shoulder. She released something that had been locked down. She identified what wasn't working—his right leg was still jammed up into his hip socket, and his ribs on the right side were compressed. She worked to open them up and address those issues. She accomplished incredible things that had not been addressed yet in physical therapy.

It truly took a village to achieve every tiny milestone, just like the progress with his range of motion in the beginning. Despite these advances, we couldn't yet move things fully back into structural alignment because of the toning in his muscles. So, we began seeing another out-of-the-box expert in their field to release that tension.

Shane's recovery involved muscle groups working against him—some were overworked, while others were underutilized. Melissa became key in helping release the knotted, overworked muscles. She was another essential player in our arsenal outside of brain injury rehab, alongside oxygen therapy, oils, hippotherapy, occupational therapy, physical therapy, speech therapy, education, counseling, and more.

Early on at CNS, Shane spoke to a counselor about his purpose and acceptance of his situation. His words brought tears to the counselor's eyes. Shane, though still recovering, continued to minister to others. While many patients were grappling with anger or questioning why, Shane stayed focused on getting better. He wasn't angry—he was determined.

We prayed for him to lean into his faith so he could keep moving forward. There was no time for self-pity or reflection. Shane stepped up for himself and embraced the arduous journey ahead. Watching him inspire others was fantastic.

He even made the two-hour drive to and from Stephenville without complaint, always keeping his eyes on the goal. On days off, we'd often fit Melissa into the schedule by running to wherever she was, combining her treatments with hippotherapy, church, and nights in his own bed.

Our days were full throttle—23 hours focused on staying compliant and committed to recovery.

LOOK UP

"They shall not labor in vain, Nor bring forth children for trouble;
For they shall be the descendants of the blessed of the Lord,
And their offspring with them.":
—Isaiah 65:23

Those extra outside-the-box modalities to keep improving were priceless. When we took him back to the therapist, I knew that the team appreciated it because then they could move on to the next thing. It wasn't unusual to hear from the therapists that Shane was progressing at a record pace. We were so encouraged by their feedback, as well as the joking and fun that always seemed to be there.

Before we left CNS, Ligia had a collage canvas picture made for Shane. On the back, she wrote him a heartfelt note, knowing he was about to transfer to outpatient therapy in Fort Worth.

It said:

Was it a coincidence that we ended up working with each other? As you know, when you were admitted, my caseload was full.

I was ever so lucky to get the boy, the OT fretted. Did you hear? He fired his previous OT. But all that, all teasing and jokes aside for that, I'm grateful.

For me, for the first time I met you, I told myself, this guy, really? He isn't going to fire me.

I'm going to fire him. Now, don't let me get your head too big. And I mean it, but during this process, you've been my sunshine and one of my biggest challenges is driving me at work.

You are so simple, Shane Hadley. And yet, at the same time, ever so complex. Like I've told you many times, I see you 51.

I've got to know you well. As a person and as a friend, it's your tenacity, your bravery, courage, kindness, honesty, and God-fearing spirit that I most love and admire about you. None of those, by the way, have to do with your strength.

Just saying, Shane, I thank you for trusting me. Okay. I suppose your uncontrollable laughter, playfulness, sass, and smart-assness are qualities too.

Shane, I thank you for trusting me in your journey and for putting up with my need for quality, or as you once stated with a bit of annoyance, detail-oriented. Well, it takes two.

So thank you. The eye rolls, the grimaces, the one upper lines, the deep sighs, the judgy head shakes, the giggles at my expense, the infamous "I'm sorrys," and "I swears," and yes, but my bruised feet were worth all of it to me.

Remember the time you told me to calm down and put your hand up to me in front of Dr. Loy? So embarrassing.

You, boy, are a mess, and somehow scored in my heart. Imagine that. Before you get bored and say your other infamous line, what's the point? Remember, it's the little things that make the biggest difference.

Those little things get mighty improvements or blessings. The motivation to the possibilities is awaiting you. God is good, Shane, and He hasn't finished with you yet.

I believe this for you.
Isaiah 41:10

Always love you.
Shane's OT,
Ligia

And P.S. Sir, you've just been fired, Finito!

CHAPTER 7
WE'RE OUT OF HERE

*"Fear not, for I am with you; Be not dismayed, for I am your God.
I will strengthen you and, Yes, I will help you,
I will uphold you with My righteous right hand."*
—Isaiah 41:10

Next was a new challenge. He would move home, but it would require him to be driven to Glen Rose, which is 33 miles from our house on the back road, and then go via cab from there to the facility in Ft Worth because there was no bus from our direction from Stephenville. No matter, over 10 months of extensive healing and therapy after the accident, Shane was able to go home to stay! *Look out, cowboy. We're riding horses again. We're moving on to a new facility.* With the Holy Spirit's guidance, we were given more equipment and outside tools. We were excited to have Shane home full time, seeing it had been over 10 months of starting from scratch physically to now since the accident. Plus, it gave us a little more free time because it granted him a bit more independence. Of course, it was scary to send him in the cab the first few times, but it was empowering that he was well enough to get his own lunch, do his stuff, and be gone for the day—even in his wheelchair. That said, he was a bull in a China closet, the way he would bang around in that thing.

My goodness, steer wrestlers and football players are not afraid to crash into things.

We had some bumps and some bruises and some broken things, but thankfully, our house was equipped for him to get around easily and do all that he needed to do without it being brought to his attention that he couldn't. We kept him so busy, though, and it was a lot. It was a lot of driving too. It was an hour and a half both ways, so he was on the road at least three hours a day—but at least he was getting well! He was walking well as the therapists worked hard to help him progress. They did the therapy they needed to do. They polished things in occupational and physical therapy.

He graduated from educational therapy because there wasn't anything else to review. His business degree from Tarleton started to fire on all cylinders. He was able to focus on the deficits that he was still encountering.

Shane was stable enough to transition from the wheelchair to a walker for good. However, his balance was still quite questionable. If he started moving backward, he was going down! As he put it, he had to master the art of the tuck and roll. Getting him to consistently use the walker was a challenge—he was still a bit unsteady.

Despite the difficulties, Shane was glad to be moving and walking on his own. There were many moments of solace, like the first time we went out purely for fun. He walked into the Stephenville Pro Rodeo on his own, using the walker—not a wheelchair. He was talking full throttle but still hard to understand. His peers saw the progress he had made, another significant step in his healing. It was emotional therapy for him, though watching the rodeo was bittersweet, as he still longed to participate.

Shane wanted to be part of that world again, and we weren't going to take that dream away or discourage him. He was still working hard to get well.

Once he was out of the wheelchair, Shane decided it should be donated back to Baylor Rehab, the place where he had been fitted for it. He wanted someone who couldn't afford one to have it. So, off we went to Baylor in Dallas to give it back.

We got to see our crew that we absolutely adored—not all of them—but Cindy and Elsie, and the therapists, Kat, Lorraine, Pam, and Andrea, and even beautiful Dr. Dubiel. Tears were in most of their eyes to see him walking on his own because they worked so hard and didn't know if he would make it out of the wheelchair. It was truly an unforgettable moment to take the time and fulfill the words that were spoken into existence, just like God spoke the universe into existence. *Let there be light.* Well, when Mr. Fox came and prayed over my son at JPS and said that he would walk out of there, guess what we did?

After dropping off the wheelchair, we went by JPS Hospital in Fort Worth and asked if Dr. Gandhi was on call. Unfortunately, he wasn't, but maybe that was a God thing. In the meantime, Shane walked into that building and, by his own will, walked out of JPS. He did what had been spoken and prayed over him—a modern-day prophecy fulfilled! If no one had spoken those words over him, would it have ever come to pass? I'm not willing to find out.

The facts show that you have to speak about things that are not as though they are—the things you hope for but haven't yet seen. What do you hope for? What do you pray for? Speak it, ask for it, and believe it's possible.

I simply asked God to bless my son with complete healing, but looking back now, I realize that wasn't big enough. I should have spoken healing over the entire family and everyone affected by this accident. Think bigger. Pray bigger. He has blessed me.

> **"Let us therefore come boldly to the throne of grace, that we may obtain mercy and find grace to help in time of need."**
> **—Hebrews 4:16**

God has blessed me, and I'm thanking Him for it. You can thank Him for your blessings, too, even before they fully arrive.

Shane was healed in the name of Jesus. We proclaimed it from the beginning, even when the healing hadn't yet come to pass. We just kept saying it. We spoke about things that were not as though they were, and that's the hope we lived in—speaking blessings while expecting God's miracles to work.

When God gives you something different than what you expected, don't respond with bitterness. I don't want to hear it because He has a better plan. You're human—you don't know everything.

We can fight it all we want. We can let frustration take over, allowing the enemy to use it to torture us. Or we can choose not to question and instead trust that God's plan is better. If you don't walk in that grace and mindset, the enemy can trick you into going down endless rabbit holes of negativity and despair.

Don't speak those things over yourself. If you don't want something to happen, don't keep speaking it. For example, if you wake up and say, *I feel so bad,* by the time you finish saying it, you likely will feel that way. Now, what else will you say?

When I met people on the streets, even when I was hurting as deeply as a mom can hurt, you know what we chose to say? *I'm blessed and grateful.*

Was I grateful Shane was hurt? Oh, heavens no. But how could I not feel blessed watching his comeback? The blessing was in the healing. Both Shane and I were blessed by the outpouring of help and support from everyone around us.

I know many moms haven't had the chance I did, and I am humbled. I have friends and family members who have lost loved ones. My niece and nephew were lost tragically and far too soon. I've seen the real pain of watching it go the other way.

Yet, we have to cling to the promises of God, witnessing His work and speaking life into existence. There were so many moments orchestrated by God for His glory and Shane's healing, and I got to watch my son ***walk*** out of JPS!

The next challenge was getting Shane out of the walker. He was going to walk on his own, but there were still things he wasn't ready for. This is where the balance between reality and speaking blessings had to align. Shane was impatient, wanting to heal faster, but one side of his body was still overcompensating for the side that was hardly working at all.

When he landed in the arena that day—with one eye open and one eye shut—it symbolized the reality of his situation. It was a complete brain sheer in which one side of his brain and the other side were torn, and the pathways described by the doctor as "shattered."

The right side of the brain controls the left side of the body, and the left side controls the right, both striving for normalcy. Shane decided he wanted to try running, but his working leg overcompensated, lifting too high and working too hard, while the other leg dragged behind. When his overworking leg landed, he broke his ankle. Unbeknownst to us, he had been outside, taking it upon himself to try running.

He called me on my cell phone. Knowing he was at home, I was confused. *Why is Shane calling?* I thought. When I answered, he said, "Well, I think I've broken my ankle." And he had.

Suddenly, we were back in surgery, with plates and screws being put into his ankle. Shane was reprimanded, but in response, he flatly refused to go back into his wheelchair. Can you blame him? He had just gotten out of it!

Thankfully, Jill Cde Baca, ever the hero, sent Shane a knee scooter so he could keep moving. Spoiled rotten by everyone, he used the scooter until he could bear weight on his ankle again. Eventually, his ankle healed, but by then, Shane had begun to truly feel the pain of realizing his body could no longer perform as it once had. He couldn't imagine crawling off a horse, grabbing a steer by the horns, or wrestling it to the ground with the athleticism, quickness, and reaction time required for the event. It was devastating.

The guilt of trying to make that steer wrestling run happen weighed heavily on him. It was a Catch-22 moment: Shane was getting well, but the reality of his physical limitations was setting in.

Sure, he was still meeting goals at a record pace. However, the incline of progress wasn't as steep, and the milestones weren't as dramatic. He wasn't plateauing, but the moments of fanfare had diminished, leaving Shane frustrated with his limitations. The more he strove for perfection as an athlete, the more the pain of his hindrances consumed him.

We had to counter that frustration with a strong mental game. To keep progressing, we reminded ourselves that physical, mental, and spiritual growth were all essential. If you don't embrace change in all those areas, you're deceiving yourself. We guarded our hearts and minds with the Scripture found in Philippians 4:6-7. Verse 8 followed as a guiding principle: *Think only on things that are true, noble, just, pure, lovely, good, and praiseworthy, and meditate on them.*

By definition, *meditate* means to engage in mental exercise, repeating a mantra to reach a heightened level of spiritual awareness. That Scripture became our anchor in navigating the journey.

It wasn't just his body. Shane had to heal physically, mentally, and spiritually. It was like he woke up from that tragedy in a young man's body, but he was somewhat of a newborn in all forms, starting from scratch, except in actual physical form. He had to cram decades of growth and learning in just months and a few years. All we could do was keep pushing to the point of progress, starting with new challenges, like adding the roping dummy to his and Barrie's riding sessions. They roped the dummy and rode in between for days at CNS, driving back and forth. Even still, his restlessness of wanting it all right then was felt.

I felt Shane's impatience almost to the point of ungratefulness, which I met him with. "Shane, you will be thankful, and we will show you the reasons why you have cause to be and where you have been. You must appreciate how far you've come and appreciate that there are others who have been hurt like yourself who haven't done the things that you have." We have a precious friend, Tim Malm, in Wyoming, who had a horse accident over a decade ago, and at this moment, he's still trying to take his first independent walk.

If Shane ever remotely considered having a pity party, I was quick to remind him, "Really, you want to go call Tim and talk to him about it?" Not to diminish Tim's progress, but we know what he has been praying to God for—independent steps.

The reason it was such tough love was because I didn't want the enemy to steal away moments of wasted time with things that weren't beneficial, self-pity being one of them. I mean, if you wallow in it enough, it will have you so defeated you can't move forward. You're paralyzed in fear, doubt, and dysfunction. Neither Shane nor Tim would represent God like that. Tim regularly preaches God's Word, shares his personal testimony, and talks about his journey in entrepreneurship through his coffee company. He also highlights his accomplishments as an inspirational speaker while trusting in God's timing for his next steps.

Let your *yes* be *yes* by believing in Jesus all the time. Belief doesn't take a break or a pause. You don't get all the worldly evidence handed to you—you get to believe. That's your part—there's no need to go back and forth on it.

What Shane was dealt was tough love. *Suck it up. Don't you dare feel sorry for yourself. Be grateful for what you have, and keep working to get better. If you want better, then work for it. Do your therapy, follow your professional team's guidance, and don't cut corners.*

It was a hard sell at times, convincing Shane to do things he didn't believe were purposeful. Eventually, even we agreed with him on some points. He reached a point where he was blowing through his therapy sessions at the Centre for Neuro Skills so quickly that they kept him busy with dominoes and games. I remember the day he came home and said, "I'm blowing through rehab, and I can't stay there if they're just going to have me playing games."

It made him angry—most of it stemming from his inability to perform perfectly and his pain from not fully accepting his limitations yet. That frustration hindered his progress and hurt deeply. No wonder God says the joy of the Lord is our strength—because anger isn't. Anger puts you in a weakened state.

When we finally agreed it was time to move Shane home completely and start doing our own rehab, it was a relief—a moment we had prayed for. We were ready to focus on places we hadn't yet fully utilized and dive deeper into the healing process.

And still, through it all, there was Jill and the *One Hit Away Foundation*.

LOOK UP

Jill, along with Dr. Sergio F. Azzolino in San Francisco, was waiting in the wings with cutting-edge equipment, innovative ideas, and new therapies to incorporate. Stopping CNS wasn't the end of the mission. When we left that place, we weren't done—not by a long shot. As far as we were concerned, we were just getting started.

> *"Be kindly affectionate to one another with brotherly love, in honor giving preference to one another; not lagging in diligence, fervent in spirit, serving the Lord; rejoicing in hope, patient in tribulation, continuing steadfastly in prayer, distributing to the needs of the saints, given to hospitality."*
> **—Romans 12:10-13**

The next place we went didn't take insurance. But thanks to scholarships from the *One Hit Away Foundation* and the incredible generosity of the Motley and Lambert families, it was possible. They had organized a hugely successful barrel race benefit in memory of Shane's surrogate grandmother, Jody Motley. This chosen family blessed Shane just as they had blessed me during tough times. We love them deeply and remain endlessly grateful.

Because of their care and support, we had opportunities that others didn't. Dr. Azzolino's expertise in San Francisco became an option, as did access to advanced equipment we'd never seen before, like the gyroscope. Jill Cde Baca went above and beyond, even putting Jim and Shane up in her father's home. She personally transported them into the city, just as she had done for other brain injury patients. Shane was fortunate to benefit from her expertise and use these innovative modalities to restore balance and even out his brain function.

Jim and Shane went out first to see Jill and Dr. Azzolino, and Shane and I followed on another trip. Jill was such a hands-on blessing, navigating the city and making extraordinary efforts to ensure Shane received the care he needed.

Finding the right people and resources for extra healing doesn't happen unless you actively seek them out. It takes finding the "Jills" of the world—people who make extraordinary things happen out of tragedies. We give thanks to our great friends Troy and Katie Scott for that connection with Jill.

Being our own best advocates and questioning the norm—whether it's for cancer, Parkinson's, or brain injury—is the best way to care for ourselves. This doesn't mean dismissing traditional advice or treatments, but there's nothing wrong with looking beyond them. Oxygen, plant essences, frequency, light, and motion—all these natural elements have been proven beneficial, yet they can't be patented or controlled by Big Pharma.

Today, we are no longer seen as the sick being made well; instead, we are treated as consumers for profit. After doctors share their expertise, it's worth asking, *Is this the best we've got?* If it were, there wouldn't be people like Dr. Azzolino out there proving otherwise. I pray for a significant shift within the FDA and the entire healthcare system to embrace more God-given holistic and innovative approaches.

Still filled with gratitude, we were thankful that Dr. Azzolino had taken his chiropractic education to an entirely new level, integrating functional neurological aid in using every possible innovation to help Shane's body heal as God intended—fully and completely. God gives us the wisdom and knowledge to defeat the enemy and provides ways to help the body function as He designed it.

Surgeons may cut the skin and stitch it back together, but true healing comes from the miraculous workings of God's creation. The body was designed by God to heal itself, and I firmly believe that all healing ultimately comes from Him.

I also believe that God expects us to be His hands and feet, using the resources He placed on this earth for healing—plants, frequency, light, motion, and other natural elements of His creation. Why wouldn't oxygen, which is essential for life, also play a role in healing? It's disheartening that we can't utilize it more effectively to enhance human health and wellness.

The reason behind this limitation is clear to me: the root of all evil—money. The flaws in the medical, insurance, food, and pharmaceutical industries reveal where priorities lie. Because these systems are often jaded by profit, we must take on the role of advocates for ourselves, seeking the best medication or therapy tailored to our individual needs rather than accepting a one-size-fits-all approach.

We're grateful we resisted the drugs they initially wanted Shane on and instead followed Jill's guidance. Her expertise led us to Dr. Azzolino and Dr. Tom, both of whom were dedicated to achieving real results. Without Jill's influence, we wouldn't have had these incredible opportunities.

We're moving forward, climbing higher, and we're not done yet. Keep looking up, everyone—we're about to get busy!

CHAPTER 8
DON'T WEAKEN NOW

> *"But those who wait on the Lord shall renew their strength,*
> *they shall mount up with wings like eagles, they shall run*
> *and not be weary, they shall walk and not faint."*
> —Isaiah 40:31

During the time we made visits to Dr. Azzolino, we were faced with the battle of staying focused and full of hope. We had to remember what has sustained us our whole journey—the *Praise Reports*! We had been using them as a tool in battle—not only to pass the time but to remember how much was going right. If something was important enough to record, it was important enough to remember. We didn't recount the horrors; those were to be remembered no more.

Like Jesus and God with our sins, He tells us, *"I'm not going to remember that stuff."* Paul, the author of most of the New Testament, went from persecuting Christians and being blind to being confronted with the choice to believe in Jesus. After that, he became a great witness and one of the most influential authors after Jesus's time on earth.

Paul was never confronted by Jesus until after His death on the cross and His ascension into heaven. While Paul was physically blind for a time, after his healing, he truly saw—in every way.

In a way, Shane's hardships mirrored Paul's. Shane was fighting his own battle, on the brink of restoration. He was asking God for a lot, but restoration always follows hardship.

> *"He answered and said, 'Whether He is a sinner,*
> *or not I do not know. One thing I know;*
> *that though I was blind, now I see.'"*
> —John 9:25

Another verse in the Bible says, *"First, brothers and sisters, I do not consider that I have made it my own yet. (Philippians 3:13)"* One thing that I do is forget what lies behind, and I reach forward to what lies ahead. I press on forward to the goal, the prize of the upward call of God in Christ Jesus. God was going to use Shane for a purpose: to stay here and show his miracles. I don't want to mislead anyone in any way, but when you serve a God that has created you, and He's glorifying you in the human instance of vulnerability, your prize and your purpose are definitely in Him, and you must show that to everybody else.

We can all have the same hope, the same opportunity to unlock those handcuffs that keep any person from believing in what God can do. The heavenly prize is when you know that no matter death, you have the promises of heaven. It'll be okay.

Even with voices trying to silence Scripture and discredit its relevance, this is nothing new. God's chosen people and His Word have been under scrutiny in many different ways throughout history.

Thankfully we have been given the opportunity to learn the Scriptures for ourselves and to believe in what Christ died to give us. When we know why and what we believe, it will help us endure the darkest moments in life. It will sustain us.

Paul wasn't relieved from being in prison or beaten, but hear me clearly—when you know where you're headed, when you know you will be rid of all that pain, it changes everything. In the place where there is no more pain, no more tears, and where you will live eternally with your Maker and Creator, that hope is as powerful as it gets. It's a hope for a world free of sin, a world where there's nothing to fear. In that eternal peace, all fear will disappear, and the peace that surpasses all understanding will fill your heart.

You can trust in Jesus, and you can look forward to the things that are present in front of you instead of staying locked into what happened in the past or might happen in the future. We would get through this. The past is unchangeable; it's about what you make of it.

LOOK UP

Shane had finally accomplished enough that he was starting to see the incline as less steep. The goals were being met, but not with as much fanfare as before. It was easy to recognize milestones like getting rid of the wheelchair or transitioning out of the walker. But after breaking his ankle, the isolation and realization of his physical limitations forced Shane to confront a hard truth—he was most likely never going to achieve the dreams he once held so dearly.

Reality was setting in. What could he rely on now? We couldn't afford to look back or cling to what could have been. As John Wayne famously said, *"Looking back is a bad habit."* We resolved to press forward because we refused to be done. When Shane's anger surfaced, we met it with advocacy —even if that meant advocating against his own self-doubt. We wouldn't allow his inability to perform as he once had to become a tool for the enemy to torture his mind.

Still, it was hard for Shane not to believe he should already be back to doing everything he used to. In his eyes, he should have been fully recovered by now—he wanted it all back immediately. The limitations on his performance deeply frustrated him, and he had little patience with himself. The truth was that Shane still had a lot to work through, and we all had to navigate that journey together.

It is what it is, and what it was—filled with purpose—had led him to the reality of what's next. The question became, *What are you going to do next? What are you going to fill it with?* There are countless examples of people who've faced much harder circumstances yet still pushed through. Even though Shane had been through a lot, he had to rise to another level. He needed to armor up every day. *Look up, Shane.* He had to confront it. And he would confront it.

The next thing he had to do was do all the extra outside of the work. Azzolino sent him home with a to-do list, so we had purpose. While at Dr. Azzolino's, we discovered that Shane's third nerve, located behind the eye, had been damaged due to being pressed or crushed against the skull during the swelling. This injury affected his speech and contributed to the trembling in his left arm, though that tremor stemmed from other issues as well.

The eyes are intricately connected to the brain through pathways essential for focus and balance. The team performed targeted brain-based therapy to address those neuropathways. Identifying the core problems— whether in life, injury, or illness—is key to finding solutions.

Now he knew why he was having the trouble that he was. You feel like you have more control when you know what the cause is. He wanted to know why his hands kept shaking. Once he had that, he could target his therapy. And so Azzolino put new wind in his sails.

Jill's heart to help was the whole connection to the wonderful news that Azzolino was telling Shane. There was lots we could do, and that was what the cowboy needed to hear! So he was in seven days of intensive therapy. Watching the doctor and assistants put in motion what we hadn't fully focused on in other facilities.

The equipment used was expensive and helpful and, therefore, not covered by insurance. The cost was relative, and without God's orchestration with the help of the rodeo community, it would have been impossible to do at this time without all the scholarship money and everyone circling the wagons to get Shane well. Shane did an aerial bike, an elliptical, things you can hardly imagine. He was coming home with all kinds of different things that he could do at home. He added a metronome app of sounds to his phone. That helped in its form. He read out loud while he was making rhythmic ticking sounds. Shane shared a daily word before the accident, and he could still share the word no longer just in a text post. We gave him the idea of monitoring his speech and improvement by recording himself in video and then serving a dual purpose. He could share his daily words, and he could film and improve his speech. We had another push.

Other items he was sent home with were these weighted ring handles to swing with the opposite knee raises to start getting more balanced and engage that core. He had belly breathing exercises that were especially for his cerebellum. All this was incorporated to be motivating and responsible for a lot of what he could do to help himself. For example, he was pushed to learn to play an instrument: piano or guitar. We were no longer going to top out with things for him to do to help. We just got a whole new list of workout stuff for him to do.

He went from being angry back to the athlete and hard worker that he always was. Jill was irreplaceable, and we can't thank her enough for all the love and everything. The tremors are not loved at all. They are a work in progress. To this day, Shane works on therapy to get them under control. At some point, you have to have a sense of humor about it and make fun of it until you can conquer it. We used humor throughout.

As we went through that, we had this new purpose and a new energy, and we were ready to do more roping and riding with Barrie. It was purposeful to get his balance. It was scary for us to watch when Shane was loping and roping, coming around that corner in heeling the roping dummy, but he kept working at it and becoming more stable. To stay in the boogie, strong and in the proper position. This journey involved finding and embracing a new purpose. It reminds me of Proverbs 17:22, which says, *"A happy heart is good medicine, and a joyful mind causes healing, but a broken spirit dries up the bones."* I watched it happen. I felt it.

There were moments when we could have leveled out, dried up, and become lost in despair. But Shane would regain a cheerful spirit and get back to speaking God's Word to everyone. In the season of waiting, give to others what you need. If you want something, go give it to someone else. It's not unlike the story of the two Jameses sent out by Jesus. They were tasked with doing what Jesus had been doing—healing people. At the time, one of the Jameses was still crippled himself. He needed the very healing he was sent to give. Imagine that!

I find it so profound that Jesus could have healed James immediately. He could have simply walked up to him, said, *"James, you're healed,"* and sent him on his way, making his journey easier. But instead, Jesus chose to send James out to give others what he himself needed. Of course, many people would have talked about James's healing if it had happened right away. But how much more powerful is it that thousands of years later, we're still talking about the remarkable act of a man giving to others what he so desperately needed himself? Well, that's what we told Shane to do. *Get out there and give everybody some kind of healing that they are in need of while you wait for what you need yourself.* Beautiful!

Later, James got his healing. God is so good, and so are His people. The Bible tells us God is ever faithful, and how powerful is it that He did that the way he did? Shane was strong for Jesus, for James, and for those hurting around him. The power that comes from getting your mind off your problems helps the mind to be strong, believing that God didn't do these miracles just for any of us to be mediocre. He does the hope-filled restoration for His benefit—to have those who love Him love helping Him back.

Praise your Lord. Hit your knees and know your purpose, to recognize that apart from Him, we can do nothing in comparison. He most definitely deserves a thank you. Thank you for another day. Thank you for allowing us to be a witness to somebody else.

So, guess what? Shane kept pushing on. We didn't weaken, and we looked up. The next goal he wanted was to drive a motorized vehicle! We started with the golf cart here and drove it throughout our place. And he, you know, is not unlike the roping. It's scary. You just pray for the best reaction time. The left hand was shaking, and there were some little bumps and bruises, but nothing major—it was progress. The pasture was full of trees and served as a useful obstacle course to practice with.

He finally pushed and pushed—nearly to the point of obsession—until Shane was ready to take and pass his driving test! This accomplishment gave him even more independence and was one of Momma Nancy's favorite milestones for him. We looked up and thought, *Oh no, he really is loose now!* Shane did get tired, though, and couldn't drive very far. But he could be "Hey Somebody" and head into town to run errands! His initial driving radius was about an hour. After that, the concentration required to handle all the stimuli would exhaust him. Still, he passed the test and drove better than most of us. He was always considered a cautious, "little old man" driver, so he was good to go.

The Department of Public Safety deemed him safe for the road, and he had no issues meeting their standards. His accomplishment came just in time for his new purpose: supporting *Cowboys Helping Cowboys*. This organization had stepped in to help Shane during a period of financial stress, funding therapies that weren't covered by insurance. Chancey Williams and the Younger Brothers Band had previously played at one of their benefits. The year before Shane got hurt, we had gone to watch them perform, as Chancey's cousin, James Williams, is married to our niece, Stephanie.

The following year, after Shane's injury, Chancey reached out to Dave Samsel with *Cowboys Helping Cowboys* and asked if they would consider Shane as one of their beneficiaries, especially if Chancey returned as the entertainment for their fundraiser golf tournament. They agreed, and the only thing ever asked of Shane was to come back and support the organization.

This support came at a crucial stage in Shane's recovery, and we couldn't thank the people in that wonderful organization enough. Every year, we make it a point to attend their golf tournament or other events.

Inevitably, Shane was the *Rockstar* he always was—just like in therapy—making everyone smile and glad to be there. He gave them hope as they saw the tangible results of their donations and generosity. Shane told everyone he was blessed and grateful, even as he limped over to speak in front of them, his deficits on full display. Dave asked Shane to share what the organization meant to him and how their support had helped him and other Cowboys. Shane spoke with humility and gratitude, showing the impact their kindness had on his recovery journey.

After Shane spoke, there wasn't a dry eye left in the house. I don't think there was a closed wallet either. They raised so much money that night. Numerous people were so moved by Shane's stories that the bands, more than once, have donated their checks back. The head sponsors were agreeing to sign contracts for another five years. People were really touched by seeing the evidence of the fruits of their labor and their blessing to those in need in real time. They got to see that he was still fighting and he wasn't asking for any more money for himself, but for others in need. Shane was asking on stage to please give it to somebody else that really needs their blessing and to have the hope and the means to do what CHC did for him. He told them, "Hey, I'm in therapy, but it's thanks to y'all that I'm able to go do some of these things."

He has gone on to speak at many events, and the same reaction happens every time he gets a microphone in his hand.

After helping raise lots of assistance for others, the founders inducted him into the Ring of Honor for being such a blessing back to their organization. With that, one is able to see how God can use anyone, no matter the condition they are in. It's a call and a purpose. I encourage each and every one of us to take what we do have and use it to glorify God. Use the excellence that He placed only in you for you to use.

And my God shall supply all your need according to His riches in glory by Christ Jesus."
—**Philippians 4:19 NKJV**

If it's cleaning the bathroom floor—glorify. Make it the cleanest one that's ever been shined up. And if it's to own the building that that bathroom is in, make sure it's run with the care and the guidance of the good Lord above like none other.

There's a responsibility at every level and in every part that we play. When one works, and you do your work unto God, it's of His best qualities in action through us because God is excellence. His power of blessing is essential to who He is—love. Let His love for us show His glory. Those who believe in Him and seek what He died to give us are the reason we strive for excellence in everything we do—whether in our rodeo events, our writing, or any other endeavor. It's why we show care for our families, work diligently at our jobs, do the dishes, and handle the tasks that often go unnoticed. When we do these things unto the Lord, they're not just jobs. They're not burdens. They become energizing and empowering because His yoke is light.

"For my yoke is easy and my burden is light."
—**Matthew 11:30**

His burden is light for us. Not because we don't have to do it for ourselves, but because He makes it joyful. The joy of the Lord is our strength. He gives us ability, and He gives us the wisdom to do even better. Where is all that strength coming from? It's coming from our striving for good—our desire to push forward with purpose. We're encouraging the cowboy to be glad, happy, and joy-filled so that he remains strengthened from within. We serve our Healer, whether we're completely healed or not.

Jim and I have gone from doing chores and tasks for Shane to now seeing him back on his feet, helping his mama saddle her horse, and getting her back in the saddle. This is happening because I'm about to face another round of that pesky ovarian cancer. And through it all, we're rescuing each other.

As I watch Shane take his roping and everything he does as a form of therapy, it reminds us to never give up hope. We won't let the experts tell Shane that he'll top out in recovery in five years. From the beginning, we didn't believe the stats they gave us, and we're certainly not relying on them now.

Take any signs of depression, change it into what you can be purposeful in, accept where you're at, and find peace and a new purpose. He may no longer be steer wrestling, but he's still a cowboy. We tease him and say now he's just a team roper. In the rodeo world, we're all known to tease one another. While roping, he is getting what we call "pretty wolfy" back there. Catchy, meaning his catch percentages were outnumbering his miss percentages. There's a way for him to get a medical exemption with special stipulations that would allow him to compete in a numbered handicapped team roping system. This system gives people of different levels the chance to rope according to their assigned number, which reflects their current ability. The association evaluates everyone on a constant basis to make sure it's fair for all. Shane is striving to get an exemption for the age limit that restricts when you're allowed to start tying onto the saddle horn instead of having to dally. This privilege is usually reserved for women and older ropers, mainly for safety reasons, as dallying can be risky given the reaction time needed in certain situations.

We've found a new purpose in not having to give up that rodeo competitive spirit. Does Shane have to let go of some specific goals he once had? Absolutely. But as he's always said, once we came to the realization and worked through the pain of it, the truth is that he's been hurt. Yet, in his pain, he is glorifying God and bringing more people to know Jesus than he ever would have by winning a championship in any arena, rodeo, or otherwise. The key is to find a new purpose. Don't let diversion or difficulty stop you from moving forward. Know where you're headed—and that it's *up*. God has bigger plans for overcoming, and He has ways to inspire you to be the best version of yourself that you could never have imagined. That promise:

> *"Now to Him who is able to do exceedingly abundantly above all that we ask or think, according to the power that works in us."*
> **—Ephesians 3:20**

It doesn't have to be what others are doing. Just because someone is, say, growing tomatoes, that doesn't mean you are supposed to grow them. The last thing you need to be doing is what God has somebody else in mind to do. The eye can't do what the nose can do, and the nose can't do what the ear can do, but everyone doing their thing brings wholeness to each part. Run your own race. Do your own thing! God will have you do something else that is designed for no one else but you to do.

In comparison, you have a fingerprint that is unique to you and you alone that no one else has. We are the same in Christ but used in our uniqueness. When you look at your own race, you are not distracted. You handle what's been placed in front of you, and you shine through any obstacle that's been placed ahead. Look up towards the bright future God has in store solely and uniquely for you.

CHAPTER 9
SURRENDER ALL

*"Therefore, submit to God. Resist the devil
and he will flee from you."*
—James 4:7

We begin to see the surrender and stand on the faith that all things will continue to turn upward. Shane definitely found a way to fill his tank back up, and we had to keep it humble.

It wasn't about Shane. It was about speaking the blessing of God's Word because he was doing it all by the grace of God and the Holy Spirit that resides in him. Not to mention, we are best used by God because, in our flaws and cracks, He does His best work. It's through our imperfections that people can see our past flaws and, more importantly, see the light of Christ shining through us. Galatians 2:20 tells us, *"I have been crucified with Christ; it is no longer I who live, but Christ lives in me."* Our weaknesses and brokenness draw attention to Jesus' characteristics in us. Shane was so broken, but yet, with the help of so many people across the U.S. and beyond, our answered prayers were shining brightly.

There was a stranger that my niece Robin, who was always there for Shane, met in Utah at a Young Living Essential Oil Conference, the oils that we were slathering on him and keeping him well from the beginning.

Nancy McCain and the rest of us recall the smells of healing from Shane's room, from those essential oils being used. As you walked down the hall to his room, you knew where he was in the building from the smell, and you could feel the healing in the air. Shane and I were in Fort Worth. My niece Robin was stepping onto an elevator in Utah with a very beautiful man, Pastor Zeke, who is a pastor in Frisco, just north of Dallas. Robin was on the phone with me at the time, and she said, "T-Bug, I think I have to get off the phone right now."

I said, "All right, I'll talk to you later."

So Robin began speaking with Pastor Zeke, sharing our story. He was flying back home, and somehow, this stranger—Pastor Zeke—flew into DFW and came to find Shane. I'm not sure what we were doing at the time; a family member was sitting in for us for a bit, and I don't remember where Jim and I were. But Pastor Zeke showed up at Shane's hospital room during one of his most painful moments at Select and prayed over him. No big deal—just God's people going out of their way to bless and pray over a stranger.

Doing better on a later date, Shane got to walk into Pastor Zeke's church and enjoy one of his services with the congregation, which had been praying for him early on. It was another one of those beautiful moments that Robin brought together by listening to that voice inside of her that said, *I don't know why I'm doing this, but I think I've got to do this.* When you listen to that inner voice of caution or that push to go help, or just stay in tune with the promptings you feel, I like to give credit to the Holy Spirit in me because I know I am nothing without some sort of divine guidance.

Be in tune. Look up. Look around. God can use you anytime, anywhere, to bless and be an unexpected blessing. That's what Pastor Zeke represented to our family. And it was just another of Robin's beautiful moments that she brought to the table.

As Shane started to surrender to his new life as a team roper instead of a steer wrestler, he also found ways to give back. He was beginning to understand how many people had come together to support him—strangers from the rodeo world, family members, non-family members—all pouring into his healing in different ways: financially, emotionally, physically, with their skills, whatever they had to offer for the journey. All their efforts went toward his improvements, including getting that medical exemption so he could participate in team roping without dallying. This was a way to prove God's faithfulness in hearing our prayers for health.

By participating in the team roping world, Shane found his avenue to keep going, saying, *I didn't give up, and they didn't keep me off a horse.* Were we worried? Well, shoot, yeah—we know the risks. Everything we do in the rodeo world is dangerous, given what can happen. But Shane's athleticism required for steer wrestling is different from the skills needed to be competitive in a numbered team roping competition.

Never ceasing to keep things real, we don't do anything that isn't rooted in the truth of God. You can't somehow believe that testing God is acceptable—just like when satan tempted Jesus, saying, *"Hey, jump off this thing. You won't even die."* Satan is a liar.

Jesus replied, *"You're not supposed to test God. Get behind me, Satan."*

> *"And Jesus answered and said to him, 'Get behind Me, Satan! For it is written, You shall worship the Lord your God, and Him only you shall serve.'"*
> —**Luke 4:8**

You really do have to confront and attack those thoughts that invade your mind because, as John 10:10 says, that's where the battlefield lies—your mind. The enemy's tactic is subtle; he changes just one word, as he did when he said, *"Surely you won't die."* His goal is to make you question everything.

Confusion is one of his most powerful weapons. The enemy seeks to enter our minds to steal, kill, and destroy. So how do you refute him? With the Word of God. You stand on the truth: *"Thou shalt not tempt the Lord our God,"* and *"He will supply all my needs according to His riches in Christ Jesus."*

> *"Yes, you yourselves know that these hands have provided for my necessities, and for those who were with me."*
> —**Acts 20:34**

We dug in. We stood on the promises of God. We cited these prayers over us. We spoke about these things that are not to be as they may.

God can bless us if we truly believe that He is capable. In 2 Corinthians, it says: *"Blessed be the God and Father of our Lord Jesus Christ, the Father of mercies and the God of all comfort, who comforts us in all our affliction, so that we may be able to comfort those who are in any affliction, with the comfort with which we ourselves are comforted by God."*

This calls us to be rivers, not reservoirs—receiving the comfort that comes from knowing the Word of God and standing on His truth, instead of allowing negative thoughts to take root and create battles in our minds.

When you know the truth and stand on His promises, you can pass that comfort and strength on to others. You're blessed to be a blessing. Shane embodied this, even while he was still in pain and not yet fully restored.

We never referred to him as "hurt." Instead, we said he was blessed and *a healing in progress.* We spoke those words over him, again and again, until we saw him work hard to make them a reality, proving wrong all the things Dr. Gandhi said would never be possible.

Today, Shane stands as proof positive that the expert was wrong in this case. Shane has taken Isaiah 43, which tells us that God is going to do a new thing. That's what Shane did. He embraced that new thing and took pride in it. He didn't hang on to the things that passed—those things he had no control over and couldn't go back and change from that fateful day. There was absolutely no option to do that, so the next step was to work with his Healer. Speak His written Word.

> *"Behold, I will do a new thing, Now it shall spring forth;*
> *Shall you not know it? I will even make a road*
> *in the wilderness. And rivers in the desert."*
> **—Isaiah 43:19**

It's now springing up. Do you not perceive it? I'm making a way in the wilderness and streams in the wasteland. There's an example in the Bible where Elijah was sent to places where he knew the creek would dry up. Just like for us, at the end of July, that water in the creek won't run anymore—it's done for the summer. Elijah was in places where God had to sustain him. Ravens, the most selfish birds on the planet, brought him food! They brought him meat. If you don't think God can use any resource, even the most unlikely one—like ravens, who don't like to share—bringing Elijah provision, you're missing it. God provided a way in the wilderness and streams in the wasteland.

As God uses you in ways you may not understand, you might feel compelled to ask, *"You're gonna send me where?"* But you have to trust. God is probably thinking, *Yeah, don't worry about it. I've got you.* You've got to trust Him. We all do. Lean on that, instead of responding with doubt, saying, *Oh God, I hope so,* putting Him back in the handcuffs of your unbelief. And He waits patiently, hoping that your faith will be released so He can take care of you—because He does care for you. God is hoping you will turn to Him.

I don't know how to emphasize enough how much your *yes* has to be *yes,* and your *no* has to be *no.* When you read what the Bible says, and you know better, you don't go back and forth, mulling it over in your mind, wondering if it's true or not. Don't waste your time with the world.

When you read the Bible, you should simply believe it's true—or why are you bothering reading it? Is it some futile attempt to disprove God? Good luck with that! I'm telling you, there has to be a decision because the enemy will keep testing even the greatest believers, trying to make people struggle and struggle and struggle. And then it becomes, *I just don't know... I just... oh.*

Well, perhaps they haven't decided what the worst thing that can happen is. Death is not the worst thing that can happen. The worst thing is that you can't believe what those promises in God's Word tell you, and that you won't have the eternity it speaks of. That's the worst thing that can happen.

Equip yourself with every good Word. Armor up, and use what it says.

There's a reason you need a helmet. You've got to protect your head. He gives you a helmet in the armor of God. With the breastplate, you need protection for your heart—because people will come for your heart. Satan will come for your heart. Put that breastplate on. Hold up your shield of faith. Those fiery darts will come from everywhere, but you hold that shield up and let them bounce right off. With your truth belt...oh boy, keep that tight. Walk in the truth as God sees it to prevent going down any rabbit holes the enemy can use against you. Stay real. Stay honest with yourself. No matter how painful it is, use that saying that goes, "You'll never know how strong you are until being strong is the only choice you have."

The degree to which a person can grow is directly proportional to the amount of truth they can accept without running away from it. So don't run away from that truth.

Read about all your armor in Ephesians 6. Tighten that belt and declare, *God's got me.* Those shoes of peace aren't there to guarantee a life free of conflict or battles. Be honest with yourself! The shoes of peace are essential because whether you're confronting something, removing yourself from a situation, standing your ground, moving forward, or running to Jesus, you can remain at peace. You know who you're serving, and you know who's fighting alongside you. *You know who's got you.*

In verse 12, we're reminded that the real battle is *"not against flesh and blood, but against principalities, against powers, against the rulers of the darkness of this age, against spiritual hosts of wickedness in the heavenly places"* (NKJV). Take a moment to absorb that. The battle is not just with people—it's with the forces at work in them: who's ruling over their heart, mind, and emotions.

This brings the question: Who's ruling over you? Which team do you want to be on? The one walking in love or the one perpetuating wickedness and torment? The choice is yours.

Now, notice something about the armor of God—there's not a single piece that covers your back. You're not meant to run away. You're meant to run *to* the battlefield.

Think of David and Goliath. Here's a young boy armed with just a few smooth stones, about to face a giant. He didn't hesitate or think, *Oh God, I hope I can do this.* No, David ran quickly to the battlefield, fully confident in the power of God.

> *"So it was, when the Philistine arose and came and drew near to meet David, that David hurried and ran toward the army to meet the Philistine."*
> **—1 Samuel 17:48 NKJV**

He didn't run from it. And that's why there's no armor to protect your backside—it's not where we're headed.

Not to be slighted, do not forget that sword—the sword you're going to fight with, the one you're going to use to cut every stinking lie away. It's the sword of the Spirit, which is the Word of God. And Jesus is the Word in the flesh.

> *"The Word which God sent to the children of Israel, preaching peace through Jesus Christ—He is Lord of all."*
> **—Acts 10:36**

That's all you have to withstand everything that comes against you. Slicing through the truth, you can call out the lies that satan will surely try to use. Respond with a powerful "Nope, God's Word says this. Period. Get behind us, satan." Cutting right through what's right and what's wrong, you have to choose to stand on God's side and be unmovable in that decision. If you start crawling back and forth over the proverbial fence, that's an easy way to get splinters in your privates.

I was blessed that my son lived and I could fight for his life. I've been with moms who didn't get that opportunity. We had to run to the feet of Jesus and thank Him for the promises of heaven, knowing we would see our little cowboy again and that he was riding horses with Jesus. That's what my friend Annette's son, little six-year-old Eddie Shane—named after me and born the same age as Shane Hadley—experienced. He was six years old when he went to get a bucket on the other side of his trailer. The horse spooked from the trailer tied next to their rig, kicked him in the chest, and killed him.

My friend, Annette, has stood on God's Word and brought me closer to Jesus in her pain than anyone else in my life. Annette's been there since we were kids, long before I lost my dad at age 16. So, do we know how to handle death? Oh yes, full-on, straightforward—thank you, Jesus, for heaven. But while we're here, don't live in misplaced blame. Put on your battle gear, know who you are in Christ, and know that you have a God who wants to save you, who wants you to be well.

He wants to give you a better life than you can ever imagine or hope for. Think about that for a second. If there's a Scripture and a promise in the Bible that says He wants to give us more than we can imagine, then take a moment to let that sink in. Allow your mind, your body, your flesh —everything that's resisting—to release hope in something you can't yet see. In doing so, you're opening yourself to the greatest blessings that God can bestow upon you.

Am I telling you that you'll never have a bad moment or a valley to walk through? No. Absolutely not. The more you seek Christ, the more the enemy may come against you. We're living proof of that. Worry more if he's leaving you alone.

How did we survive being kicked off the family ranch after Jim had devoted six decades of his life to it? I'm not trying to be disparaging, but let's go with the facts. Let's keep this belt of truth tight, right? We've had to face some difficult realities—like not knowing where to live, losing our vehicle, having no job, and watching our son and daughter try to graduate from college while their parents were going through all of this. There's been so much resistance. Before Shane got hurt, I was already going through cancer. And shortly after that, we discovered Jim was struggling with Parkinson's.

It hasn't been easy. But writing it down for everyone today, I can admit that surviving all of this will be worth the glory of being used by God to give others hope. It's humbling in every way.

We can't help but laugh because we really are like that old country western song, where everything that has happened is just like the lyrics. Except, of course, they'll never steal our Bible or kick us down. We're still standing.

We've refused to give in, and we're not giving up. We'll continue to protect and shield our loved ones from pain. That's the kind of cowgirl warrior mentality it takes to resist the enemy coming against you and your family. Shane is still being guided by that same drive, that same spirit, and that same Word that pushes us to be all that God expects us to be. And there's fulfillment in knowing you gave it your all, even if it wasn't perfect. That kind of fortitude can only come from God. He loves us, flaws and all. It doesn't hinder His mission in the slightest—and, in fact, He kind of prefers us to be dependent on Him and Him alone.

When you truly know in your heart that you're trying and giving your best, then nothing anyone says or does can deter you from what God has placed in front of you. The true gratitude from those listening to Shane's devotionals online was evident. He received a lot of feedback—good, encouraging feedback—showing that his efforts were reaching people and making a difference by sharing Scripture and expanding his thoughts on what they mean to him.

People, complete strangers in a nearby restaurant, would walk up to our table and ask, "Are you Shane Hadley? Are you the one who does devotionals? I really enjoy them." Love that for him, but immediately don't let your flesh take credit for that. It's the Holy Spirit that has enabled you to share that good Word of God, and you let it keep glorifying God and serving its purpose—not yours. Don't worry about how many likes or comments you get. Stay humble. Don't lose sight of who you're doing it for and why you're doing it, and you'll remain steadfast.

I think it's easier not to get caught up in the entangled webs of different motivations that can lead you astray and steal your joy in a heartbeat. Because once you start seeking approval or recognition, you're no longer doing it for the right purposes. You've shifted to trying to fill the void in your flesh where you're hurting. We've all been guilty of it; we've all done it. But allowing God to use you for His purpose is so much stronger, better, and more fulfilling. And when you do that, you won't be living in the hurt of the hardships the enemy tries to throw at you.

Keep it reeled in—there will be new troubles of their own each day. Some minor, some not. Our battle's still going on, but it's changing. The challenges are changing. Passing through all those valleys, don't worry, God has a plan to help you out. You may not get it immediately, but you'll get it in time. That's a guarantee. God is never late. He's never early. He's always right on time. When you're in the middle of all the mess, remember that the only way out is through. You're rising up out of it, just like getting beauty for ashes, as it says in Isaiah 61.

As we watched Shane get going with Melissa, he and she did the bodywork, and now, he's doing more and more for us—helping his family, even pushing his sister's calf every once in a while, like the days of old.

We got the selfless Shane back in rare form. Not completely, but we got him doing what Shane does—blessed to be a blessing. Finding purpose and helping others as much as he's been helped. It's looking like it's endless.

There is a way to continue this—to help people with brain injuries or any ailment. A way to show them that they can have more hope than the status quo allows—more hope than what the system permits them to believe. Most importantly, they don't have to rely solely on what they tell you, but on what you're willing to do with God's help.

There's a prayer that was sent to us:

Today is my day for a miracle. I will keep looking up and forward. For I am blessed. I am highly favored by a great God. I will not let negative thoughts occupy me one ounce of my life. I am secure, sane, and full of joy. I am moving forward. I declare this shall be a day of awesome opportunities that will outweigh any and every obstacle that may try to hinder my purpose. I am walking in extreme favor. In Jesus' name, amen.

Amen.

You hear those statements, those things that haven't happened yet in someone's life. If you're praying for a miracle, you're in the trenches. When you're in need of a miracle, the situation is as dire as it gets, and you're forced to call on God.

Do you need a miracle? Speak of things that are not as though they are. That's faith in action. Instead of waiting for the miracle to happen before thanking God, start thanking Him now for what you believe is already done. That's what I did from the very beginning. *Thank you, Lord, my son is healed. Thank you, Lord, for healing Shane.*

That prayer didn't start when we brought him home. It started in the first facility. It began while I was praying he would one day make it back home to sleep in his own bed.

I remember coming home for a brief day—the first time I'd been home since the accident. I walked into the house, saw his empty bed, and felt the weight of the situation. Shane was still gravely injured, and I caught myself thinking, *I hope he makes it back to that bed.* I don't know if I said it exactly that way, but it was a fleeting twinge of fear, a moment when satan tried to slip in doubt and make me question the possibility.

The enemy wanted me to believe Shane might never come home. But the advice was the same then as it is now: *Look up. Our God is good and faithful.*

I rebuked that horrible thought and pressed forward. Although Shane didn't come home immediately—months and months passed before that moment—we endured through God's strength and patience.

Shane's journey required countless hours of physical therapy and evidence of progress, inch by inch. Slowly, through faith and perseverance, the miracle of life and healing came to pass. *Don't lose heart. Stay in your Bible. Let the Word sustain you.* You can just keep repeating over and over all day long. There's one for whatever you're going through. And that's when you realize what it truly means to pray without ceasing—speaking and applying the Word nonstop. Simply realize that God can hear you, see you. He's with you through accepting Christ and taking help from the Holy Spirit's guidance from your faith in Jesus. My part is to release that power; I don't have to want it. I know I possess what He promised to give me by believing in Him and not handcuffing Him with my doubt, with my words. Life or death is in the tongue. You can speak blessings or cursings over yourself. You have to decide.

> **"Death and life are in the tongue, And those who love it will eat of its fruit."**
> **—Proverbs 18:21 NKJV**

I taught Sunday school when the kids were in school. And the mantra that I made those high schoolers say to me is, "I choose." Because they had to choose to do what was right.

They choose to believe or not. They will have to choose to stand on the promises of God. It's a choice. So when somebody says they don't have any choice, I don't believe that; that's wrong. You have a choice to believe or not. You have a choice to accept it or not.

You have a choice to surrender and have faith in something that you can't touch or not. And like I said, it sure makes it easier if you just go ahead and do it, so you never have to look back. You don't come back across that fence. It's over. *I believe in Jesus. I believe what this Word says. There's nothing y'all can do to me to make me believe otherwise.* And if you don't want to stand up in that kind of no backup whatsoever, then I tell you, I pray for you, the torment that the enemy will do with you. So I don't say it lightly when I say don't back up on this.

LOOK UP

*"The spirit of the Lord God is upon me because the Lord has anointed me
To preach good tidings to the poor; He has sent me to heal the
brokenhearted, to proclaim liberty to captives, and
the opening of the prison to those who are bound."*
—Isaiah 61:1

You believe in Jesus, and you don't back down. I just hope that Shane realizes how much all had to come together, but I suppose I know that he already did.

I know everyone sees that there's no way one human could have accomplished this—that it was only by the grace of God and all the things that had to come together. We witnessed a huge, beautiful miracle that began as the worst nightmare any mother could imagine. Seeing God work through it is something that should be shouted from the rooftops.

Some of the most encouraging words Shane received were from his football coach at Chadron, Coach Bill O'Boyle. While he sent several messages, I'll sum them up with the following:

> *Shane, I wish this team had one ounce of your determination and toughness! Keep busting your ass in rehab! Love the progress you've made and know the future is bright. Keep that Classic Rock rolling and stay strong!... As always, you're a true inspiration! Keep up the great work (and readings)... I had an OL (offensive line) sleeveless hoodie for you to show off those guns. Take care of yourself, and know you're welcome.*
>
> *Love ya, Shane!*
> *Bill O'Boyle*

Coach sent gear and cheer and left him with the greatest work ethic and attitude of any coach that Shane had. We are so grateful for your support, Coach O'B! You keep your guys tough and keep rocking in the free world!

Our family does and will continue to be forever grateful. We thank God every day for giving us second chances that others, I guess, seemingly sometimes do not get, for giving us the opportunity to be that light that shines in a dark world where nobody wants to be brave enough to stand up and say, *I'll show our God is real.*

TRINA POWERS-HADLEY

PASTOR WERTH MAYES'S LETTER

"What is happening, Lord?"

"Just watch...that is all I have asked you to do, just watch."

Shane was slowly making his way past the tables in the back. He was shuffling past the people. His eyes were fixed on me. I could not hold back the tears. Shane was responding to the invitation I had given following my sermon. I always pray for the Holy Spirit to speak, to touch, to move people to action. Could this be real? No one was helping him or holding him. No walker. Shane was walking down the long center aisle of the church. I could not move, just watch. Our entire church was weeping as we witnessed a miracle. We had prayed, we had believed. It was here. It was here in our midst. In some ways, it had been so long. Yet, I can still hear the telephone ringing beside my bed that night.

When my phone rings at midnight or later, it is never good. The voice on the other end was shaky. "Shane had been in a bull-dogging wreck. The steer cut in front of his horse. They have careflighted him to John Peter Smith Hospital in Fort Worth. You need to get here fast, it's bad." I hung up and began to pray. I felt my wife's hand on me. "Who is it, what has happened?" she asked. I told her it was Shane, and it was bad. I didn't have a good feeling about it. As I drove to the hospital, the feeling just got worse.

I walked in and found the family and friends. No one was talking. They took me back to Shane. It was bad. Shane was bad. Still, no one spoke. I am not sure how long we stood there—it felt like hours. I had no words. Words sometimes just fall short. Words were not needed; words would not help. As if the Holy Spirit had prompted each one of us, we grasped hands. All I could get out was a cry for help. "God, only You can save him. Please God, do what only You can do." The words were not eloquent or deep, but the theology was not wrong. From a place of complete helplessness, a desperate cry to God was lifted up. I heard, or I thought I heard, "Just watch."

The road was long, always hard, and often tedious. Yet, God was working. Shane would prove the doctors wrong time and time again. In the hospitals, in the physical rehabs, I kept hearing the words, "Just watch." His determination was unmatched, except for that of his family, especially his mother, Trina. Yeah, though I walk through the valley, we speak of valleys with such euphemism, until we are there. Our valleys show us who we are and what we are really capable or not capable of accomplishing. Our valleys, more importantly, show us God. We learn not to just lean on Him, but to fully depend on Him. We learn to receive, we learn to submit, we learn God's grace. We come through the valleys changed. We come out stronger. We come out heralds as we are eyewitnesses of God's love and care. We hear His words, "Just watch."

I don't have any problems showing my Jesus. And that's a call that comes not for the faint of heart or for the self-conscious. It comes for the ones that are boldly running to the battlefield going, *Here I am, God. Use me.* So when you look up and you thank God for all that He has given you, He will give you more than you can ever dream or imagine. Believe and don't quit before the miracle happens. Heroes don't die—they make it to the finish line. Jesus said it is finished.

CONCLUSION

*"Now to Him who is able to do exceedingly abundantly
above all that we ask or think, according
to the power that works in us,"*
—Ephesians 3:20

Have you ever truly wondered why the world is so quick to champion almost anything or anyone, no matter how bizarre, yet works tirelessly to diminish one person more fervently and consistently than anyone else in all of human history—Jesus?

Society often tries to slight Him, using tactics designed to distract from the purity and truth of His story. Diversion is everywhere, often disguised as "all in good fun." For instance, the celebration of Santa and exchanging gifts takes the focus off the glorious birth of Jesus. Meanwhile, the Easter Bunny hops away with the most amazing news—life after death!

The story of Jesus brings a way to reconnect with God and live eternally with Him, as He intended from the very beginning, before the fall in Genesis.

The sugarcoating of things like Halloween with ghouls and such to overshadow All Saints Day—any diversion to take the focus off the eternal, to place it on the earthly, the finite. Don't slight or be distracted from

God without first giving Him the glory. It's that simple: Nothing should come before Him. That is what was put on my heart. And this truth solidifies the case that Jesus is God in the flesh, and the fallen angel enemy can't stand the Truth and the Light in our presence because it gives us the freedom to choose the hope we have in our belief and faith in our Creator.

Jesus—seriously? This is who they think is too terrible to talk about in public, with His message of love for all people, compared to someone like, say, the devil—scantily clad, gyrating on a big stage for the world to see? Give this Christian cowgirl a break! The enemy seeks to make people uncomfortable talking about Jesus. However, my perspective highlights why those most preoccupied with the fleeting concerns of this world—such as misleading media, Hollywood, or the latest political correctness agenda—are part of an evolving plot to hinder the Good News of the Gospel.

The Maker of all things embodies love, joy, peace, patience, kindness, goodness, gentleness, faithfulness, and self-control—the Fruits of the Holy Spirit (Galatians 5:22-23). There is little downside to believing in these virtues, for they are truly worth embracing.

I encourage a call to arms to become the enemy's greatest modern-day opposition. Someone once coined the phrase "Do it afraid" to inspire action. I say, look higher—do it fearlessly.

"Then they said to Him, 'What shall we do that we may work the works of God?' Jesus answered and said to them, 'This is the work of God that you believe in Him whom He sent.'"
—John 6:28-29

Don't let the Bible—made up of those 66 books compiled over all these years—intimidate you. God shares the history of creation, His people, and what works and what doesn't. In the Old Testament, they point you to a savior—Jesus. The New Testament tells you about the one who was nothing like what they thought He should be. Let the truth of the Lord transform you into the best version of yourself, as He intended. It's our hope that all will be blessed and know they are loved.

On a more personal note, our finish line is out in front of us with the latest in brain injury therapy, thanks to Dr. Kyle Daigle in Lake Charles, Louisiana. His profound new results, coupled with inventive laser technology, have led him to speak and teach all over, with this therapy showing even more targeted results. As a past TBI patient himself, he is a wealth of knowledge that other doctors can't provide. There's no doubt his approach is the biggest recent advancement in therapy. His experience is so valued that royal families in Dubai are seeking him out to help build a practice in their country. Unfortunately, he's often snubbed by the approval of insurance within the medical establishment. However, with months of saved disability checks, we are hopeful that Shane can attend therapy regularly. We know that God will provide the means for this, and we are confident that Daigle and his team are key to a brighter future. Keep those shades handy!

There's no help like cowboy help, and we cannot thank you enough for the care that has made this healing possible. Shane's story is a success because of every person who has prayed, invested, and used their talents and love to help. Life's a dance—do you stay on the sidelines, or do you "stay in the boogie?" Shane reminds us every day to "stay in the boogie" because the only way out is through, and the only way we're going is up.

He has formed a nonprofit, the Look to Faith Foundation, to help others in need. Let's do great and mighty things in His Name—the name above all names, Jesus Christ. Amen!

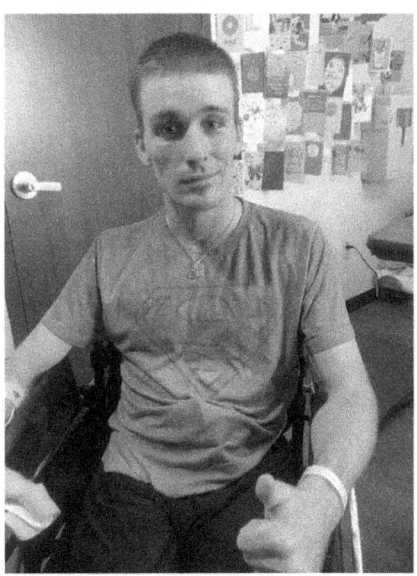

Shane at his third facility (the much-hoped-for Balor Rehab) after his third feeding tube placement, surrounded by his walls of encouragement cards.

Shane on his horse, Buckwheat. Shane was there when he was born and imprinted him as a colt (before the accident), but didn't see him until years later (after the accident). Over half a decade after the accident, Buckwheat is taking care of him like nothing else we have ever witnessed with our horses.

THANK YOU FOR READING MY BOOK!

As a token of my gratitude for buying and reading my book, I invite you to visit <u>looktofaith.com</u> for a chance to put faces to the names of some of the wonderful people involved in Shane's healing journey. The website is dedicated to his nonprofit foundation. There, you can click on the *Look Up* book extras to view photos from his actual journey.

In addition, you'll find the foundation's mission statement and scriptural encouragement for the future. Shane's attitude of hope reminds us that we are blessed to be a blessing—helping those in need, just as he was helped. He is truly motivated to live out Galatians 6:2: *"Bear one another's burdens, and so fulfill the law of Christ."*

Scan the QR Code

I appreciate your interest in my book, and value your feedback as it helps me improve future versions of this book. I would appreciate it if you could leave your invaluable review on Amazon.com with your feedback. Thank you!

www.ingramcontent.com/pod-product-compliance
Lightning Source LLC
LaVergne TN
LVHW041337080426
835512LV00006B/505